WITH

WOLVES

WRESTLES

WITH

WOLVES

SAVING THE WORLD ONE SPECIES AT A TIME
A MEMOIR

BILL KONSTANT

Archimedes' Printing Shoppe & Sundry Goodes

FSC certfied and printed in support of Trees for the Future
with soy-based, eco-friendly inks in China.

Cover and Interior Design by A Little Graphix
Adrianna, Bebas Neue, Garamond, Marydale, Permanent Marker Pro, Superclarendon

Photos by author or Konstant family, unless otherwise noted. All photos are copyrighted
by the respective holders. Edited by Lucy Noland, Peggy Jackson, Dr. Allison Alberts and
Dr. Anthony B. Rylands. Thanks to Paula Katharina Rylands for foundational design work.

Library of Congress Cataloging-in-Publication Data
LCCN: 2022912708 | ISBN: 978-1-7372851-2-0
Classification: LCC QL31 .K66 2022 | DDC 798.4/0092--dc23
Names: Konstant, William R., author. | Mittermeier, Russell A., foreword author.
Title: Wrestles with wolves : saving the world one species at a time, a memoir /
Bill Konstant; foreword by Dr. Russell A. Mittermeier.

Summary: A wildlife conservationist who describes his life as
"Mowgli meets Forrest Gump" takes us on the wild ride that is
his legendary career. *Wrestles With Wolves* is an adventurous
trek to the frontlines of animal conservation that is at
once touching, inspiring and funny.

Subjects: Wildlife conservationists—Biography |
Environmentalists—Biography | Wildlife conservation
| Personal Memoirs | Biography & Autobiography
| Environmentalists & Naturalists

13 12 11 10 9 8 7 6 5 4 3 2 1
First Edition.

Archimedes' Printing Shoppe
& Sundry Goodes

re:wild

life
lifesaving initiative funding efforts

صندوق محمد بن زايد
للمحافظة على الكائنات الحية
The Mohamed bin Zayed SPECIES CONSERVATION FUND

for **MOM**
who taught me
how and when
to swear

and

for **DAD**
who often
made me want to.

CONTENTS

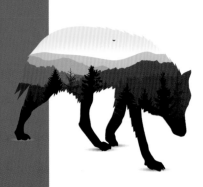

RUSS MITTERMEIER AND ME, THE HOUSTON ZOO, 2017
PHOTO COURTESY OF HIROMI TADA

FOREWORD

I've had the pleasure of working closely with Bill Konstant for more than 40 years. We've traveled together to many countries, hiking through tropical forests and deserts in search of rare species, speaking to colleagues and donors at special events, and sitting around the conference table deciding how best to help other wildlife conservationists in their tireless efforts to save the world's threatened plants and animals from extinction.

Bill's friendship and collaboration are special to me on many levels. This was evident to everyone in the room a couple of years ago during my acceptance speech for the prestigious 2018 Indianapolis Prize—the world's leading award for animal conservation. After the speech, having just sat down at the head table, I felt Bill's hand on my shoulder. He thanked me for acknowledging his help through the years, emphasizing that I just happened to reference his name three times, while no other friend or colleague was mentioned more than once. Vintage Bill. I wasn't aware that I had done so, but the truth is our accomplishments together are that memorable and noteworthy.

I first met Bill in 1980 at what was then my office in the Department of Anatomical Sciences at Stony Brook University in New York. He recounts the story early in this book, so I won't steal his thunder here. Suffice it to say we hit it off immediately. And why not? We were both Long Islanders with similar educational backgrounds from Ivy League schools (he at Cornell and me at Dartmouth), and we were both passionate about animals. Bill recently reminded me of something I told him at the time: that I saw my life and career as climbing a very tall ladder, cradling as many endangered species as I could manage in my arms, not willing to allow even one to fall and disappear into the abyss of extinction. My fantasy actually does drive my actions daily and still serves as an inspiration for Bill who has done amazing things with many organizations in his long and diverse career.

As chairman of the IUCN Species Survival Commission's Primate Specialist Group when we met, I soon invited Bill to be a member, and he continues to serve to this day. Together, we started many important programs and projects, including the Primate Action Fund, which has supported thousands of projects for emerging primatologists around the world.

Bill seems to have a tolerance level of roughly five-year cycles working directly for me after which he "takes a break" and goes to work at another organization, but we never lose touch. He first left my employ as a program assistant at the World Wildlife Fund to take the executive director's post at the Wildlife Preservation Trust International, the American arm of the late Gerald Durrell's Jersey Wildlife Preservation Trust.

When I became president of Conservation International in 1989, Bill joined me once again. At that organization, we worked together to build a strong primate conservation program and launch a series of publications that prioritized countries and regions for biodiversity conservation. In 1996, having "gotten sick of me" once again, Bill moved to the Philadelphia Zoo where he created One With Nature, that institution's first conservation program. That same year, in collaboration with several colleagues, Bill and I launched the Margot Marsh Biodiversity Foundation with a generous gift from the late Margot Marsh of La Jolla, California. Bill accepted the task of managing the Foundation's scientific advisory committee and grant program, a role in which he has faithfully served to this day. During that time, we have awarded close to 700 grants totaling more than $15 million to primate conservationists around the world.

In 2003, I "loaned" Bill half-time to the newly privatized Houston Zoo, where he worked with his longtime friend and fellow Cornellian, Rick Barongi, to develop a global wildlife conservation program. Rick had worked previously at the San Diego Zoo and then for the Walt Disney Company, where he was instrumental in the creation of Disney's Animal Kingdom Theme Park. The three of us fellow Long Islanders have been friends for many years. Bill's stint in Houston lasted a predictable five years after which it obviously was time for him to seek a new challenge.

In 2008, when a generous gift from the Crown Prince of Abu Dhabi enabled creation of the Mohamed bin Zayed Species Conservation Fund, I was asked to organize an advisory board. So who did I choose once again to help manage grant-making activities for this important new body? That would be Bill, whose attention focuses principally on securing the future for rare and endangered mammals. To date, the Fund has awarded more than 2,150 grants totaling more than $20 million, helping to ensure the survival of nearly 1,400 species and subspecies of mammals, birds, reptiles, amphibians, fish, invertebrates, plants and fungi.

In 2017, after 28 years at Conservation International, I moved to a young and dynamic organization called Global Wildlife Conservation (renamed Re:wild in 2021), founded by its CEO, Wes Sechrest, another conservation visionary. In 2020, Bill was invited aboard as a senior associate with a special focus on primates.

Why do I always look to Bill when opportunities arise that promise greater support for species conservation? Simply because he is one of the most talented, creative, and dependable people I have ever known. His passion for nature stems from early childhood experiences and has grown enormously through the many personal and professional relationships that he's established through the years. Bill is a team player with an undying sense of humor, even in desperate situations. If he accepts a difficult task, I can always count on his best efforts and a laser focus on achieving the maximum conservation impact. I, of course, must then tolerate a string of jokes, puns and gags that seemingly has no end. But that's his way of dealing with tasks that many others might find daunting. However, should I have to listen to even one more of his mother-in-law jokes, I may become seriously ill.

Every now and then, I'll kid Bill about his moves from one organization to another after only a few years. He takes my ribbing in good humor, as it's intended, but isn't shy about explaining his work philosophy. He has zero interest in severance pay, pensions or gold watches and will never see himself as a "company man." Instead, with whomever he happens to be working at the time, he likens himself to a catalyst in a chemical reaction—necessary to boost the energy to the next quantum level, but not required when the final product emerges. It's an interesting rationale and actually makes a good deal of sense.

In *Wrestles With Wolves*, Bill weaves a thread through a series of life-shaping memories that continue to guide his personal and professional path into his golden years. He shares lessons learned from both the animal and human actors in his life drama, with the hope that the kindred spirits among his readers will recall or create their own stories and become more involved in efforts to preserve the wonders of the natural world.

Russell A. Mittermeier, Ph.D.
Chief Conservation Officer
Re:wild

MY SISTER DONNA AND ME, NEW YORK CITY, 1958
PHOTO COURTESY OF WARNER BROS. STUDIOS

PREFACE

Nobody abides a liar.
But everybody sure likes a good storyteller, don't they?

Lynda Rutledge, *West with Giraffes* (2021)

The inspiration for this book came from a memoir writing course offered by my local library. I had written my share of project reports, grant proposals, research papers, magazine articles, book chapters, and field guides, but I had never before tried my hand at this more creative and challenging genre.

It was our class's initial getting-to-know-one-another activity that planted the seed for this book. The instructor carefully tore up a few sheets of blank paper and passed the pieces around the table. We each took one.

She directed, "Now, I want each of you to write down, in just a few words, some fact about yourself that you don't think the rest of us will be able to guess. It can be the work you do, something that happened to you years ago, or maybe a secret that you've kept for a while and now don't mind sharing. Please don't let anyone see what you write."

Just like every other time I'd been asked to do something like this, my mind immediately went blank. I didn't start to sweat or anything like that, but it felt almost as if someone had stuck a vacuum cleaner hose in my ear and sucked out every memory I had in my skull. And then, just like every other time, it took maybe all of 60 seconds for something to bubble up from the depths. So, I jotted down three words, covered the slip of paper with my hand and looked around to see everyone else doing the same.

The instructor then said, "Now please fold your slip of paper twice over into quarters and drop it into the hat as it's passed around the table."

Everyone did as instructed.

"Okay, who'd like to pick first?" she continued.

I don't remember how many picks were made or how many of us correctly guessed which secret belonged to which classmate before someone selected my slip.

One of my classmates unfolded a scrap of paper and read aloud, "I trained chimpanzees."

We all scrutinized one another like poker players looking for their opponents' "tell." I furrowed my brow, squinted slightly, and twisted my lower lip as I scanned my classmates around the table, doing my best to look analytical. It worked.

Someone blurted out, "I think it's Stephanie!"

Several others nodded in agreement, chiming in, "Me, too!"

Someone else disagreed. "No. I think it's Steve!" Again, a few concurred, but both Stephanie and Steve shook their heads. No one noticed the sly smile spreading across my face.

Our instructor ended the suspense, "Well then, who here is our chimpanzee trainer?" I slowly raised my hand. My classmates joined in a communal smile, several clapping softly in appreciation of having been fooled.

The instructor was quick to add, "We'll have to hear more of this story from Embellishing Bill the next time we meet." I had chosen Embellishing Bill as my preferred nickname at the

KENTON AND ME, STONY BROOK UNIVERSITY, NEW YORK, 1983
PHOTO COURTESY OF ANDREW L. YOUNG

opening of the class, suggesting that I might be inclined to stretch the truth ever so slightly.

The following week in class, I read my first draft of a memoir, *Ode to a Chimp*. Based on my classmates' favorable feedback, I was confident my lifetime of adventures with creatures great and small—from family homes, in zoos, and through jungles—could become a book, no embellishment needed.

My original working title was *Of One Blood: A Zoologist's Memoir*. I had snatched the first snippet from Rudyard Kipling's *The Jungle Book*. I'd read the nineteenth-century classic as a young boy and watched the original 1942 movie production and Walt Disney's 1967 animated version on television. I joined millions of my fellow Americans who packed movie theaters for the Disney remake. In the Kipling original, Mowgli, the "Man-cub" raised by wolves, made sure to approach fellow jungle creatures with respect, reciting the greeting, "We be of one blood, ye and I."

Human beings are bona fide members of the animal kingdom. Science confirms that we share more than 95 percent of our DNA with our closest living relatives: chimpanzees, gorillas and orangutans. Surprisingly, we also share approximately 90 percent with cats, more than 80 percent with dogs, cows, and mice, and even as much as 60 percent with chickens. Perhaps even more surprisingly, geneticists tell us that chimpanzees are more closely related to humans than they are to their ape cousins. Hints to that reality emerged when I was a kid thanks to the groundbreaking field studies of Dr. Jane Goodall. Dr. Goodall had discovered that chimpanzees can fashion and use simple tools, a trait once thought to be uniquely human. She also documented bouts of aggression and violence between chimpanzee groups, suggesting that the origins of warring behavior may date back well into our primate history.

About halfway through writing my original draft, several people offered somewhat less-than-positive critiques of the working title. One friend remarked, "Of One Blood? What is it, a hematology textbook?" Another colleague cautioned me against hanging my hat on an outdated Kipling quote. I hadn't noticed that the folks at Disney had canned the phrase in their original *The Jungle Book* production. The same colleague who cautioned me against too strong a reference to Kipling was particularly taken with my story of wrestling with a young timber wolf and was drawn to a picture of me doing just that. He thought it might help conjure a more enticing title, and I think he was right.

And so my playful tussle with an ancestor of the domestic dog, little more than a snapshot in time, inspired *Wrestles With Wolves*. It is also a not-so-subtle nod to Michael Blake's classic novel turned Oscar-winning movie starring Kevin Costner. His character, Lt. Dunbar, had his own moment with a wolf called Two Socks which transformed the lieutenant into Dances With Wolves.

Humans are in a constant dance with nature. I'm what you'd call a "biophile." Professor E. O. Wilson of Harvard University coined the word "biophilia" to help explain humankind's reverence for, and inextricable link to, nature. Wilson suggested that humans are genetically hardwired to connect with the living Earth. We require closeness to our fellow creatures—not to granite, concrete, iron or steel. Wilderness is essential to our well-being. I believe nature nurtures us both spiritually and physically.

My life could easily be summed up in four words: Mowgli meets Forrest Gump. And, now that I think of it, four more words: six degrees of separation.

Over the course of my career, I've interacted closely with hundreds of fellow biophiles, including some of the most talented and dedicated people on the planet. Without question, we are a motley crew, a nimble team of zoo professionals, field biologists, college students, professors, veterinarians, artists, photographers, authors, journalists, computer geeks, television personalities, rock singers, movie stars, Tarzan wannabes, government officials, religious leaders, corporate bigwigs, soldiers, poachers-turned-rangers and assorted philanthropists. Our combined work provides the raw material for the stories in this book.

As defined by Malcolm Gladwell in his book *The Tipping Point*, I seem capable of playing two roles. At times, I play a Connector, someone who knows a lot of people and is capable of reaching out to them. Apparently, I'm also comfortable in the role, as Gladwell describes, of a Maven, an accumulator and a disseminator of knowledge. Gladwell defines both agents as being critical to generating "social epidemics" where ideas, products, messages and behaviors rapidly spread through society. I'm pleased that Gladwell further defines a Maven as not being someone likely to "twist someone's arm." That's not my style.

I also do my best to fill the role of Trickster Hero, much like the cartoon characters from my childhood—Bugs Bunny, Woody Woodpecker, and Mickey Mouse—or animals of myths and folklore like the fox, coyote, raven, and spider who enjoy bending the rules at times to make good things happen.

In the battle to save species from extinction, where talk of doom and gloom sometimes rules the day, the need for some comic relief is all too real. I'm a big fan of comedy. Even some of the more insensitive jokes can be therapeutic. One of my favorites was told by the late Buddy Hackett: "A guy said to me, 'There are only 10 snow geese left in the world.' I said, 'One craps on my car, there'll only be nine.'"

Obviously, whoever told Buddy that there were only 10 snow geese left in the world was completely misinformed. The guy's estimate was off by several orders of magnitude since there were at least a million of the birds around at the time. Hackett's friend probably was referring to the California condor, which, at its lowest point, numbered in the low double digits.

What's key here is the man's absurd reaction: his threat to kill an endangered bird that had the nerve to defecate on his car. Should I ever be asked to give a talk about successful efforts to save any of the world's endangered birds, I just might lead with this joke just to break the ice.

My hope is that those who read my stories will take them to heart, draw parallels to their own lives and become more engaged in efforts to protect the planet. In my experience, everyone knows someone who knows someone else who's already involved. It's all about my fellow biophiles identifying these connections and using them to become more involved in the cause: safeguarding the incredible variety of life on Earth. Ours is a huge team with plenty of positions in need of filling, now and into the future.

What we love to do, that we do well.
To know is not all; it is only half.
To love is the other half.

John Burroughs
Leaf and Tendril (1908)

AUTHOR'S NOTE

Several photos in this book depict me, as well as family members and colleagues, in close association with lemurs, monkeys or apes. In 2020, the IUCN SSC Primate Specialist Group put forth Best Practice Guidelines for Responsible Imagery of Non-Human Primates to help ensure that published images do not have unintended, negative consequences for primate welfare and conservation; someone viewing such an image might decide to capture or purchase a wild primate for a pet. The photos I have chosen for this book depict people whose work requires them to be in close quarters with their non-human primate cousins, either in captivity or in nature, and in no way suggest that such contact should be undertaken casually or with the intent of removing wild primates from their natural habitat.

WRESTLES

WITH

WOLVES

EASTERN BOX TURTLE

EASTERN GARTER SNAKE

PICKEREL FROG

BILLY THE KID

... the boy exhibited a spirit of reckless daring,
yet generous and tender feeling ...

Pat F. Garrett, *The Authentic Life of Billy the Kid* (1882)

I arrived in this world on October 27, 1952. According to historians, I'm a Baby Boomer. Tens of millions of us exist. We were born between 1946 and 1964. We Boomers share this label due to the unrivaled reproductive success of our parents. They're members of the so-called Silent Generation. Reportedly, historians defined them as such because of their reluctance to speak out. No historian ever met my parents.

My grandparents were members of the Greatest Generation. I was lucky. No other kid on the block had three grandmothers. Actually, two were my grandmothers and one was my great-grandmother. All of them lived on Park Avenue in North Merrick, Long Island—barely a mile from each other. There was Little Grandma, Big Grandma and Big Big Grandma, whose relative body sizes earned each of them their pet name.

Little Grandma was well under five feet tall. My great-grandmother was a member of the so-called Lost Generation, folks who came of age during World War I and the Roaring Twenties. She was a devout Catholic, rarely without a string of rosary beads in her hands and always making some reference to the Virgin Mary. Born just outside of Naples, Italy, she ended up getting pregnant out of wedlock as a teenager. Little Grandma decided to have the baby which really was the only choice a young Italian Catholic girl would have had in the late 1800s. As the story goes in my family, my great-great-grandfather

BIG BIG GRANDMA WITH DAD, NEW YORK WORLD'S FAIR, 1939

confronted the young man who had dishonored his daughter and *strongly* urged him to "do the right thing." For whatever reason, the young man declined the advice. Bad decision. He paid for it with his life. Retribution may have come with the blade of a knife or perhaps through the barrel of a gun. Who was he? No one knows and all the witnesses are long gone.

Little Grandma understood English, though she rarely spoke it. Every morning she read the entire *New York Daily News* front to back, and Heaven help anyone in the house who tried to grab

the newspaper before her. Little Grandma had big opinions, such as President Nixon really *was* a crook and *no man* ever set foot on the moon. Her feet trod this planet for 98 long and wonderful years.

Big Grandma was Little Grandma's daughter-in-law. Soaking wet, Big Grandma probably weighed all of 110 pounds, but she stood at least several inches taller than her mother-in-law, which made her Big in my book. I remember her telling me that she had worked ever since the age of five. Her first job was to gather acorns to feed the pigs. Big Grandma never struck me as a particularly religious person, except when she reminded us that "God helps those who help themselves." For more than 50 years, I can remember spending every Christmas at her house, which was the family gathering spot for most holidays. Big Grandma was the family matriarch. She was always straight to the point, had a good sense of humor and stayed that way right to the end. When asked what she wanted to do for her 99th birthday, her reply was an emphatic, "Go to the Bronx Zoo!" She died just a few months shy of 100.

At somewhere between 250 and 300 pounds, Big Big Grandma pretty much fit her pet name. Food always seemed to be within arm's reach whenever I walked down the block to visit her. It might have been because she and I often sat in the kitchen which adjoined her bedroom. I can close my eyes and see a holiday roast pig in a pan on the stove. Its skin was golden brown, shiny and crisp, and a burnt apple was wedged in its mouth. Around the corner in the pantry, right next to the refrigerator, was a two-gallon tin of Wise Potato Chips, always there for munching. Big Big Grandma's kitchen was one of the first places where I opened a book. I remember reading to her from one of my favorites: *The How and Why Wonder Book of Reptiles and Amphibians*. I doubt that she believed even half of what I read to her, and I'm sure that much of it creeped her out.

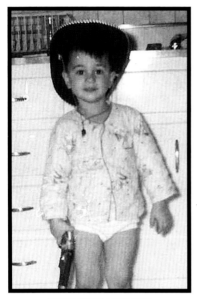

"THE YOUNG OUTLAW"
NEW YORK, 1955

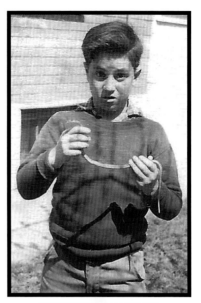

MY FIRST GARTER SNAKE
NEW YORK, 1960S

Big Big Grandma would just shake her head. "No, I don't believe it! I don't believe that a snake can swallow a pig!"

"But Grandma, here's the picture!" I didn't call her Big Big Grandma to her face or let on that my sister also referred to her that way. "You see, the boa constrictor is squeezing the pig in its coils to kill it. After the pig suffocates and dies, the snake will swallow it whole. It says so right here in the book." She'd just continue shaking her head, "No!"

"Yep, this really happens!" I'd reply. Admittedly, I had never seen a boa constrictor actually swallow a pig, but I didn't think it was impossible. "Grandma, you don't have to worry. These big snakes don't live around here, just little ones. I'm going snake hunting this summer, and Mom and Dad said I can keep any snakes I catch."

CAMPING WITH DAD, CATSKILL MOUNTAINS, NEW YORK, 1950S

"You be careful of those snakes," she warned me. "Their tongues have poison. And they can hear you coming before you even see them. They just wait and hide and then they bite you. And their poison will make you sick or even die."

"No, Grandma, snakes can't hear you. They don't have any ears!" I decided it wasn't worth arguing about snake venom, so I just turned a few pages in the book to show her a diagram of a snake's head. "They can't hear us, even when we yell really loud." I tried to explain to her that a snake's body is very sensitive to vibrations through the ground and that it certainly could sense a person's footsteps from far away. That just meant that I would have to walk slowly and softly when I went snake hunting. But she wasn't buying any of it. "When I catch a snake this summer, I'm going to bring it here to show you."

5

Big Big Grandma just smiled and offered, "How about we have something to eat?"

Nichols Estate was my favorite snake-hunting grounds; it spanned more than 600 acres of woodland, meadows and marshes. Garter snakes were everywhere. Water snakes liked the creeks; black snakes, the woods; and milk snakes, the fields closest to the barns. Hognose snakes were supposed to be around, but I never saw any, even though plenty of toads—their favorite food—were hopping around. My snake-hunting buddies and I also caught snapping turtles, box turtles, spotted turtles and leopard frogs. The private estate was a little less than two miles from my home. I'd pack a bologna sandwich and a can of Yoo-hoo for lunch then head to the home of the Walker brothers. Billy, Lee and Gary lived only a few blocks from the estate and I could always count on at least one of them to join me for a hunt.

"**Herps**" is what biologists commonly call reptiles and amphibians. Scientists have discovered at least 30 herp species within the Fire Island National Seashore's thousands of acres. Four-toed and red-backed salamanders live beneath the woodland leaf litter. Fowler's toads hop, box turtles trundle and garter snakes slither through the meadows while mud turtles, spotted turtles and snapping turtles lurk in the marshes.

The Old Mastic House stood proudly on the estate, the front door looking out onto Moriches Bay. It was the birthplace of American patriot William Floyd. He was born in 1734. Floyd served in the county militia as a young man and rose to the rank of major general during the Revolutionary War. He served as a New York State delegate to the First and Second Continental Congresses and signed the Declaration of Independence. My high school was named in his honor. I took great pride in trespassing on such prestigious property, but more so in never having been caught.

THE OLD MASTIC HOUSE, LONG ISLAND, NEW YORK, 2015

Long before I was born, William Floyd's country estate passed to one of his direct descendants, Cornelia Floyd Nichols. She was married to naturalist John Treadwell Nichols, a biologist who specialized in native amphibians, reptiles and fishes. Nichols was a curator at the American Museum of Natural History. During the week, he commuted to work in Manhattan from his home in Garden City, Long Island. Come the weekend, he and Cornelia would travel 50 miles east to their country getaway. I never did meet John Nichols, who passed away several years before my snake-hunting days. But Cornelia Nichols ...

I don't remember what possessed me to confess my years of trespassing to Mrs. Nichols. Yet at 12 years old, I summoned the courage to write her an apology letter. At the close of the letter, I even worked up the nerve to ask if I might see the inside of the Old Mastic House. Much to my delight, Mrs. Nichols wrote back. She didn't reprimand me. Instead, as I had hoped, she invited me to visit her on the weekend. She even let me bring a friend, so my cousin Michael from Brooklyn tagged along. Michael routinely spent a couple of weeks every summer with my family and had hiked the Nichols Estate with me many times. Together, over the years, we probably brought back a few pillowcases filled with turtles and snakes from our adventures—reptiles that ended up summering with us before we released them in the fall.

AMERICAN PATRIOT WILLIAM FLOYD
COURTESY OF WILLIAM FLOYD SCHOOL DISTRICT

Mrs. Nichols asked that we meet her at the kitchen door on the side of the house. She spent the bulk of her weekend on that end of the big house preparing meals. Opening the screen door, she welcomed us inside. As she untied her apron and placed it on the back of a chair, she remarked, "So, it seems you boys already know quite a bit about the natural world outside my home. For a proper tour of the inside of Old Mastic House, we really must begin in the parlor at the front door." We followed her through the kitchen and dining room and into the parlor. It felt like we were stepping out of a time machine straight into the past. The house smelled as I imagined a house would smell in the 1700s. We stood in the middle of the parlor. "I'll tell you a little secret," Mrs. Nichols whispered as she leaned down and placed a hand on each of our shoulders, "There's only one part of this house that's the same as when General Floyd lived here, and it happens to be right here in this room. Everything else in the house has been rebuilt or replaced. Can you boys look around and tell me what you think is the same today as it was nearly 200 years ago?"

STRIKINGLY-MARKED DIAMONDBACK TERRAPINS FORAGE IN BAYS
ALONG THE SEASHORE'S BARRIER ISLANDS

She stepped back and allowed us to inspect the room. We offered a few guesses. "The front door?" "That window?" "The painting on the wall?" Each time, Mrs. Nichols just smiled and gently shook her head. "No, I'm afraid you haven't found it." She placed her hands on our shoulders again, turned us toward the front door and ushered us over to a corner closet. She opened the door and pointed inside. "That's the original wallpaper, the only thing that's exactly the same as when William Floyd lived here." She stepped back again and motioned with her hand around the entire room. "When British soldiers took over the house during the Revolutionary War, they used this room as a stable for their horses. They destroyed much of what he had built and took anything of value that he had owned. It was a great insult to my great-great-grandfather."

Mrs. Nichols led Michael and me through the rest of the Old Mastic House, giving us a personal tour from cellar to attic. She pointed out her father's Civil War uniform, the same one he wore when he met President Abraham Lincoln. I remember thinking how incredibly cool this all was and how lucky Michael and I were to see all of this.

In the kitchen, he and I sat at a small table while she washed and trimmed a bowl of green beans for dinner. There, she let us in on another little secret: She had recently signed a contract that would give her house and property to the United States government in a few years. It would become part of the Fire Island National Seashore, managed by the National Park Service. My favorite snake-hunting haunts would forever be preserved, but it also meant that my days of sneaking onto the property would one day come to an end. Mrs. Nichols must have sensed my disappointment. Taking pen and paper from her desk, she jotted down something to this effect: "This note gives my permission to William Konstant, a young boy from Mastic Beach, to enter the grounds of the Floyd Estate, as long as he refrains from collecting any animals or plants." She signed the note, smiled and handed it to me, making sure I understood the consequences.

Mrs. Nichols passed away a number of years later; our paths never did cross again. I continued to hike on the estate, proof of permission in my pocket. I kept my promise and didn't catch any more animals. Come to think of it, I don't remember ever having to show my note.

Today, just as Mrs. Nichols had arranged, the country estate of William Floyd is a key component of the Fire Island National Seashore. Thanks to her foresight and generosity, more than 25 miles of beaches, dunes, maritime forests and wetlands along the barrier island that parallels the Atlantic Ocean off Long Island's eastern coast is protected in perpetuity.

LESSON LEARNED:

Our love of nature transcends generations, allowing young and old alike to participate in its protection.

IMMATURE BALD EAGLE, WILLIAM FLOYD ESTATE, MASTIC BEACH, NEW YORK, 2016

EASTERN GRAY SQUIRREL

CHIPS
ON MY SHOULDER

... after contemplating you a while unobserved,
and making up his mind that you are not dangerous,
he strikes an attitude on a branch,
and commences to quack and bark,
with an accompanying movement of his tail.

John Burroughs, *Squirrels and Other Fur-Bearers* (1875)

One summer, Mom and Dad said it was okay to let the kitchen faucet drip. We didn't consider that wasting water. You see, the kitchen sink was where the family squirrel liked to take a drink.

Yep, a squirrel was part of our family. One of the kids in the neighborhood had found the little guy lying cold on the ground in his backyard. He was so new to this world, the baby squirrel's eyes had not yet opened. Most likely, he had fallen from a nest. I don't remember the boy or his family being animal lovers, save for the fact that they had a yappy little pooch—one of those breeds that I fondly referred to as "almost a dog." I'm guessing that the boy's parents urged him to take his new "nuisance" pet down the block to my house. My neighborhood reputation as Mother Nature's son was already well established. I don't recall having before raised any animal orphans, but my family had no objection to me giving it a try.

The Konstant family was all in. My sister couldn't offer her doll's plastic baby bottle fast enough, and my parents acted as if they were adopting a third child. We named the squirrel Chips,

CHIPS AND ME IN MY TEENS, MASTIC BEACH, NEW YORK

which my mom and sister quickly prettified to Chi-Chi. His survival became our common responsibility. Chips took to the doll bottle without a fuss and survived his first weeks in the Konstant household on slightly watered-down cow's milk (which in retrospect is rather amazing since I later learned that's a no-no for most baby mammals). We found an old bird cage in the cellar, lined its bottom with shredded newspaper and placed a cardboard shoebox inside that was stuffed with strips of cloth from a torn towel that had seen better days. That's where Chips napped during the day and slept during the night between feedings. As soon as his eyes opened in the morning, he became a dynamo, so we gave him the run of the house. That worked well enough during the day, but, to ensure there were no accidents in the middle of the night, we placed him back in his little hacienda after dinner. A small supply of twigs and a box turtle shell on which he could gnaw kept his incisors nice and sharp. Thankfully, he rarely tested their sharpness on any of us.

Over the course of a few months, we weaned Chips from the milk bottle and provided a bowl of water in his cage. At some point a light bulb must have flashed inside his head; he figured out the kitchen tap provided an endless supply of fresh water. Why we never bought one of those Lixit bottles that hang upside down in hamster cages, I'll never know. We just let the faucet drip every so often during the day and he managed to drink his fill. The image remains vivid in my mind: his lithe gray body stretched along the length of the faucet with his cute pink tongue lapping up each drop as it formed at the spout. Chips wasn't particular when it came to nuts; he took any and all from our hands. He also seemed to enjoy joining the family each evening in the living room as we watched television, acting as though we were his own personal trees. He'd climb up our arms to our shoulders then jump to the tops of our heads. There, he'd smooth down our hair with his front paws, stretch himself out and slide down our foreheads. Sometimes, he'd come to a stop on your face; otherwise, he'd land in your lap.

When Chips wasn't scampering down the hallway, hiding peanuts in a fruit bowl on the kitchen table or napping in his cage, he'd often hitch a ride on our shoulders—or heads. The first day I walked out the back door with him on my shoulder, he quickly leaped up to the top of my head, began flicking his tail and chattering. Not having studied Squirrelese in school, I could only imagine what he was saying to me: "Hey, Big Fella, hold on there! Where are we going? Maybe slow it down a bit and let me get my bearings here. You may know where we're going, but I haven't got a clue!" It was his first venture back to the natural world, and I probably should have warned him.

On that first stroll under the oaks and sycamores in the backyard, his claws pierced my shirt and dug into my skin. He wasn't taking any chances of falling off. Yet, on our very next adventure, as I stopped and stood in place for just a few moments, he summoned enough courage to climb down my pant leg and test the lawn. I guess he concluded that grass was just another kind of carpet and nothing to fear. He began scurrying around with the same confidence he showed indoors, while I kept an eye out for any neighborhood cats that might be hiding in the yard and licking their lips. Pleased with his survey of this new realm, he jumped back onto my pant leg, climbed up to my shoulder, and we walked back into the house together. Time for a couple of peanuts!

One time, my family took Big Grandma *and* Chips on a family camping trip to Hershey, Pennsylvania. The little guy handled the four-hour drive extraordinarily well (if you don't count him nipping Big Grandma's knee for no apparent reason). Otherwise, he spent the drive resting on Dad's left arm as he steered with his right—Dad, not Chips. I still laugh when I think about it, having heard the irony of Dad's own squirrel story so many times over the years. (It's not quite so warm and fuzzy.)

After quitting school at the age of 14, Dad left home and headed for the hills, taking a summer job in the Catskill Mountains training trail horses. The pay was decent, just enough for him and one of his buddies to rent a room, pay the bills and feed themselves through the autumn months. When winter arrived and the riding season ended, money became scarce and the cupboard grew bare. Dad has always been resourceful. He recounted how he and his friend survived the winter on a diet of squirrels, picking off the little buggers one by one with his trusty .22-caliber rifle.

Chips wasn't fazed by Dad's story. After we arrived at the campground and pitched the tent, he happily relaxed in his bird cage while the rest of the family toured Chocolatetown and Hershey's other attractions. Had Chips decided to return to the wild while we were in camp, say, leap off the picnic table and head to the woods, nothing would have stopped him. We simply would have had to accept his decision and tearfully wish him good luck in his new life. Instead, he hung out all weekend, and we all returned home.

GRAY SQUIRREL IN MY FAMILY'S YARD

We knew the day was coming, though. I had begun taking Chips on walks in the woods behind our home, encouraging him to explore on his own. My friends got a real kick out of this. They'd come along and watch as our squirrel bounded around in the leaves and climbed high into the trees. He'd always return when I called him with my best squirrel imitation; I'd purse my lips and suck in air through my top teeth. He was a bit apprehensive of the resident squirrels at first, but soon showed no fear in scampering up to them. His time spent off my shoulder increased dramatically.

One day, Chips took interest in a particular white oak tree in the side yard. Jumping to the ground from my shoulder, he bounded to its trunk, climbed up then scurried to the end of the lowest branch. Chips began to bite off leaves, stuffing them into his mouth. He carried his bounty up the trunk to a branch near the top then wedged the leaves into a crevice with his front paws. Down the trunk he came, back to a lower branch, and he repeated the process, stripping the lower branches of leaves as his little construction project progressed. Somewhere, deep down in his squirrel brain, were the hardwired instructions for nest-building. It was pure instinct and an incredible thing to witness. I wondered if Chips imagined sleeping under the moonlight that night.

Nest construction completed, Chips shimmied down the tree trunk, scurried up my pant leg and leaped to my shoulder. I turned my head, looked him directly in the eye and asked, "Are we done now?" He stared back as if to say, "Yeah, we're done and I'm starving. Let's go inside and get something to eat." I put a few peanuts in a bowl for him while he stopped at the kitchen faucet for a drink.

Water drunk and peanuts eaten, Mother Nature's miniature engineer then followed me down the hallway to our bedroom. He climbed into his bed while I went back to the kitchen and cleaned up. By the time I returned to our bedroom, he was spread-eagle on his back in his bed. Had he begun to snore, I wouldn't have been at all surprised.

Chips' time outdoors grew longer each day. And he became bolder and more adventurous. Chips might disappear into the woods for hours at a time, but he would always return to the back door by sunset and scratch to let us know he wanted in. The first time that he failed to show up before dark we all worried that something bad had happened. The next morning, however, there he was scratching at the door. Chips hung around with us for a while that morning, but he eventually returned to his new home in the woods. He visited again a few days later, but then a week went by before he showed his cute little rodent face. Chips had turned the corner and was adapting to a new life in the wild. He was on his own, coming and going as he pleased. A bag of nuts was there in the cupboard should he stop in for

I WONDER IF CHIPS FOUND A FRIEND AFTER RETURNING TO THE WOODS?

a meal, and he knew where the kitchen sink was if he needed a drink. However, autumn came and went that year without any sign of the little guy.

One recent summer, I returned to the old neighborhood and paid a visit to an old friend who I hadn't seen in more than 50 years. When we were kids, Emil and his family lived in Brooklyn, but they spent their summers at a vacation home in Mastic Beach. Emil and I, and our friends, Frank and Phil, spent the summer months playing baseball or just hanging out. My friends got to know Chips very well. Years later, Emil, his wife and his children moved into his childhood summer home. I just happened to be driving by, so I thought I'd drop in and surprise an old friend. Walking up to the front door, I gave a knock. Silence. A car was parked in the driveway, so I tried again. The second time, I heard footsteps inside and watched the doorknob turn. The door opened slowly but by only a crack. I could make out the form of a red-haired man in his bathrobe. "Can I help you?" he asked, very likely thinking that I was selling something.

"I'm looking for Oats." No one called Emil by his given name. Some called him Red for his bright red hair. Others called him Oatmeal because it sort of rhymed with Emil. Frank, Phil and I shortened Oatmeal to Oats. So, half a century later, a white-haired man shows up at his front door and calls him by a name used only by three people many, many moons ago. It clearly caught him off guard. Oats looked me up and down, opened the door just a bit more, and was about to speak when I let him off the hook.

"It's Bill Konstant, Oats. You probably didn't recognize me with this scruffy beard." Oats just smiled, opened the front door wide and motioned me to come in. "If you had a squirrel on your shoulder, I'd 'a' known exactly who you were."

These days, just like nearly everyone else in America, my wife, Nannette, and I feed the birds that visit our backyard. And, yes, we feed the squirrels, too. In addition to whatever they manage to steal from the birds, we put out a few special squirrel treats. They need to flip the lid on one container to grab a peanut. We also set up a tiny red picnic table where they (or the resident chipmunks) can sit for a more casual meal. And, after every Halloween, the squirrels seem to take special pleasure feasting on any corncobs remaining on the stalks that decorate our front porch.

Squirrels

play a critical role in Earth's ecosystems. Consider them woodland gardeners. Gray squirrels, for instance, bury acorns, nuts and seeds; hence, they disperse oaks, walnuts, butternuts, hickories, beeches and other trees throughout the forest.

The gray squirrel is the most abundant of the North American species. In fact, back when Pennsylvania was still a British colony, gray squirrels were so plentiful and considered such agricultural pests that the Province of Pennsylvania

GRAY SQUIRREL ENJOYING A FALL TREAT IN OUR YARD

levied a threepence bounty for each one dispatched. The reward was so attractive that many farmers and laborers put down their tools and picked up their rifles since they could make more shooting squirrels than they could tilling the land or toiling in the shop. Gray squirrel relatives include the smaller red squirrel and larger fox squirrel, and the more distantly-related, aerobatic flying squirrels. Ground-dwelling relatives include chipmunks, marmots (groundhogs) and prairie dogs. Surprisingly, remaining populations of a handful of these otherwise common rodents are now considered threatened, including the Utah and Mexican prairie dogs, Palmer's chipmunk of Nevada, the Northern Idaho ground squirrel and the Vancouver Island marmot.

LESSON LEARNED:

Although young animals may be able to adapt to human lifestyles, they may also retain instincts and traits critical to their survival in the wild. I was privileged and humbled to have a young squirrel as my teacher, helping me help him return to Mother Nature's care.

PEREGRINE FALCON, WIND OVER WINGS, CONNECTICUT, 2010

⊖

THE
DOG
WHO DRANK WITH
SUPERMAN

⊖

... none do I owe so much as to Stickeen. ...
Our storm-battle for life brought him to light,
and through him as through a window
I have ever since been looking
with deeper sympathy into all my fellow mortals.

John Muir, *Stickeen: The Story of a Dog* (1909)

Kilo was our Stickeen. Our faithful and adventure-loving canine companion was a floppy-eared, shepherd mix with a penchant for chasing tennis balls. He was also a force of nature that brought together three Cornell undergraduate biology students with renowned ornithologist Dr. Thomas Cade. A conservation legend, Dr. Cade is largely responsible for saving several of North America's most threatened birds of prey: the peregrine falcon, osprey and bald eagle.

I first met Kilo in my freshman year at college. I was sitting in the laundry room, in the basement of my dormitory, waiting for the washing machine's spin cycle to end and checking my pockets to make sure I had enough quarters for the dryer. As I looked down, a saliva-covered tennis ball slowly rolled to a stop between my feet. The shepherd-mix that dropped the ball stood there in front of me, his eyes fixed on it and his tongue shooting in and out rapid-fire with each short breath. When I reached for the ball, he snatched it up in his jaws just ahead of my hand. Almost as quickly, he would drop it. And round and round we went until he finally let me pick up the soggy mess again. I pretended to throw the ball to his right. He leaned in that direction. I feigned a toss to the left; he immediately tilted that way. Finally, I got up and hurled the ball through the door, turned and sat back down. Within seconds, my new friend was again in front of me, chomping and drooling on his precious toy and ready for round two.

Kilo would do anything for a tennis ball. He'd fetch them from cascading waterfalls or even the pounding surf of the Atlantic Ocean. Each time, he'd disappear for several anxious seconds, but, without fail, he'd emerge from the spray and foam, dog paddling his way to shore, that precious piece of felt-covered rubber clamped tightly in his jaws. One time he almost leapt out of an open second-story window in hot pursuit of a tennis ball recklessly thrown by some idiot. Thankfully, an agile classmate, realizing what was about to happen, grabbed the hyperfocused dog midair.

Kilo was one of more than a dozen dogs that roamed free on the Cornell campus, back in the good old days when such things seemed normal. He actually lived off campus with a student who rented an apartment in nearby College Town. A metal tag on Kilo's collar included the guy's address and telephone number. A couple of dorm mates, both named Bob—the Bobs—returned Kilo to his home one night, having had their fill of fetch and feeling that it was past the dog's curfew. That same routine repeated several nights in a row until the owner finally asked, "Why don't you guys just keep him? He spends all his time on campus anyway."

The Bobs didn't think twice and back Kilo came with them. When the Bobs were at class, Kilo ran free on campus, fetching tennis balls—there seemed to be an endless supply of them—

KILO OUR CORNELL UNIVERSITY POOCH, 1970S

and chasing the occasional car. That was a habit we could never break. I say "we" because just about everyone on our dormitory floor shared in Kilo's adoption.

Summer had the Bobs taking Kilo north to their homes in Rochester on the shore of Lake Ontario. Kilo had the time of his life, exploring and employing his ancestral wolf roots as they hiked and camped in the Adirondack Mountains. The only drawback to their adventure, as the Bobs told it, came each night when Kilo decided to crawl into one of their sleeping bags. It was entirely his choice as to which one of their faces had the honor of sharing the space adjacent to his butt. Many nights, Kilo's long, low growls woke them, conjuring images of hungry bears and other creatures prowling about.

Sophomore year, the Bobs, several other classmates and I rented a suite of rooms on the third floor of a new dormitory. Of course, Kilo was one of the guys. Freshman year lessons were not lost on him. Instead of sneaking past the front desk on the ground floor like last year, he now climbed the fire escape, cleverly out of sight on the other side of the dorm. He'd stand on the ground and bark until one of us on the third floor opened the back door. Only then would he clamber up the stairs to be let in.

Some mornings Kilo would go off by himself to spend the day chasing tennis balls. Other mornings he'd follow one of us to class. We'd try to ditch him, but he was too clever. He actually learned our schedules. He'd take off just ahead of us and be waiting at the classroom door when we arrived. He even learned to use the elevators. He'd trot in on the ground floor when the door opened, wait patiently inside as it moved up or down, and then sniff the air when the door opened again. Eventually, he would catch our scent, exit on the correct floor, walk into class, and lie down at our feet.

Rumor has it that Kilo met Superman one day. It's said that they shared a beer. I wasn't there, so I can neither confirm nor deny the story, but I heard it from several people. Christopher Reeve, the actor who later played Superman on the big screen, was a fellow member of the Class of '74 at Cornell and easily could have been enjoying a beer at the Chapter House, a storied neighborhood pub. Kilo could have shown up there too since the hangout was well within his territory. Had Christopher Reeve poured a little beer in a bowl on the floor, I have no doubt Kilo would have lapped it up, especially if he could dip in his tennis ball to sop up the suds.

When summer rolled in after my sophomore year, I brought Kilo home with me. I was still living with my parents on Long Island. They hadn't had a dog since Queenie, a tiny Pomeranian mix whose first job was to protect me when I was a baby. Queenie would lie in wait, hidden from view, under my playpen in the backyard. If anyone other than a family member came too close, she'd leap out and bark with the ferocity of a little lion.

I inherited a passion for dogs from my father. Among my favorite family photos is one of him as a boy, wearing a pith helmet with

DAD AND LADDIE, QUEENS, NEW YORK, 1940S

Laddie, his beloved white collie, sitting alertly at his side. In the 1940s, when Dad was only 10 years old, he bought Laddie for $50, a treasure trove of money at the time, especially for a kid. Dad used the money he had saved from his job cleaning out coal ash from a blast furnace in the bowels of a boiler room. I did mention he was 10, right? He earned all of 11 cents an hour.

Every so often, Dad would retell the story of how his own father fell asleep in the living room with a lit cigarette dangling from his hand. It dropped from Grandpa's grasp onto the couch or carpet and started a fire. The smoke and flames sent Laddie running into the bedroom where he woke my grandmother— Big Big Grandma—who put out the fire. And I thought that stuff only happened in the movies.

Mom and Dad welcomed Kilo to our Mastic Beach home with open arms when I brought him home for the summer. We took turns playing fetch and they looked after him when I worked at my summer job. They even helped put an end to his habit of chasing cars by installing a chain-link fence around the backyard. Let's just say right before that fence went in, Kilo had a close encounter of the vehicular kind.

When it came time to return to school, I loaded up my trusty Volkswagen hatchback and motioned to Kilo to jump in. He just stood next to my parents in the open doorway as if he hadn't heard me. I called him again but he refused to budge. Mom and Dad stood there and waved to me, tears welling up in their eyes, not because I was leaving, they didn't want to watch Kilo bound down the front steps. Well, they didn't have to worry; he didn't. Kilo just stood beside them and wagged his tail. I didn't need to read dog lips to know what he was saying. The message was clear: "Thank you, my friend. I'll be just fine here. This is my home now. You drive safe and say 'Hi' to the guys for me."

The Bobs weren't entirely surprised when I showed up at our new digs for junior year without Kilo. To be honest, they were relieved, as we'd moved to a new dormitory called Ecology House, where it would have been much more difficult to care for our loyal companion and hide him from the authorities. Dogs were still allowed to run free on campus, but free housing for canines was a no-go. Our junior year was also destined to be particularly intense, course-wise. The Bobs and I had signed up to serve as undergraduate teaching assistants for a monster of a course called Anatomy of Vertebrates. The five-credit course included two hour-long lectures and two three-and-a-half-hour lab sessions each week. It was recommended for seniors, but we had taken it as sophomores to avoid scheduling conflicts. Little did we think we'd ace the course and be asked to help as lab assistants—an invitation we couldn't refuse.

Teaching was hard work, but it was an incredibly rewarding experience. The Bobs and I spent many a late night in the lab preparing the next day's demonstration dissections. We carefully cut into small animals to expose their nerves, muscles, blood vessels, bones and cartilage for our fellow students. We quizzed one another relentlessly to make sure we knew the subject matter cold. We'd be the ones answering questions for hours on end the following day, and we didn't want to be embarrassed.

Our first order of business was to recognize and remember the 12 cranial nerves found in all vertebrate creatures (fish, amphibians, reptiles, birds and mammals) from nose to neck:

olfactory, optic, oculomotor, trochlear, trigeminal,
abducens, facial, auditory, glossopharyngeal,
vagus, spinal accessory, hypoglossal.

The Bobs and I first learned to recite the nerves in anatomical order by memorizing the following phrase:

On old Olympus' towering top,
a Finn and German
viewed some hops.

I remember thinking that was pretty clever. Granted, the image doesn't make any sense. Why would one guy from Finland and another gentleman from Germany stand on the peak of a 10,000-foot mountain in Greece, both looking out over a field filled with plants that are essential to brewing beer? Making sense isn't the point; remembering something complex is. That's the beauty of a mnemonic device.

Cranial nerves

allow great white sharks and crocodiles to slice and tear chunks of flesh from their prey, bats and dolphins to "see" in the midnight sky and the ocean depths, and elephants to rip a tree and its roots from the earth and shower themselves at a waterhole. They're the same nerves frogs use to croak, cats to meow, dogs to bark, and humans to speak, sing or snore.

Teaching vertebrate anatomy introduced the Bobs and me to the course's lead professor, Dr. Thomas Cade. Dr. Cade had joined the Cornell faculty several years before our arrival as freshmen.

DR. TOM CADE AND PEREGRINE FALCON, CORNELL UNIVERSITY, 1968
PHOTO COURTESY OF DIVISION OF RARE AND MANUSCRIPT COLLECTIONS,
CORNELL UNIVERSITY LIBRARY

In addition to his teaching courses, he directed research at the Laboratory of Ornithology and founded The Peregrine Fund, one of the world's leading international wildlife conservation organizations. In the 1950s and 1960s, North American birds of prey were falling victim to the dreaded pesticide DDT. The numbers of breeding pairs of peregrine falcons, ospreys and bald eagles east of the Mississippi River were plummeting. Canada banned DDT in 1971; the US followed suit in 1972. Two years later, Dr. Cade and his colleagues at The Peregrine Fund began releasing captive-raised peregrines into the wild, beginning one of the most successful wildlife reintroduction initiatives in our nation's history.

At the end of the course, Dr. Cade invited all the teaching assistants to his farm in Dryden, a short drive from campus, for a barbecue. The treat of the day was meeting the different

OSPREY, MERRITT ISLAND NATIONAL WILDLIFE REFUGE, 2020

BALD EAGLE, FORT WASHINGTON STATE PARK, 2021

KWANG (B. 1965), DR. CADE'S FEMALE BATELEUR EAGLE
THE WORLD CENTER FOR BIRDS OF PREY, BOISE, IDAHO, 2021
PHOTO COURTESY OF WORLD CENTER FOR BIRDS OF PREY

hawks, falcons and eagles that lived in his barn. We each had the opportunity to handle one of the birds of prey. For a precious few minutes, a majestic bateleur eagle perched on my forearm. Bateleurs are striking creatures. The male I was holding had a coal-black head, breast and wings, a chestnut mantle, silver epaulets, a bright-red face, and a yellow-and-black-tipped bill. The now endangered eagle's range stretches across Africa, south of the Sahara Desert. I quickly gained an appreciation for its amazing strength. Had I not been wearing a gauntlet glove, standard equipment for any falconer, the bird's talons easily would have skewered my wrist. Its wingspan was longer than I was tall, yet the bird probably weighed little more than the shoes on my feet.

The eagle that perched on my arm was one of two bateleurs that lived with Dr. Cade, who passed away in 2019. As of 2022, one of the birds was still alive and well—nearly 50 years later—at the World Center for Birds of Prey in Boise, Idaho.

Although I didn't participate in the falcon breeding program while at Cornell, years later I would cross paths with Dr. Cade and members of The Peregrine Fund team on a remote island in the Indian Ocean. To this day, conservation biologists continue to work around the clock there to save several of the world's most endangered birds from extinction. But that's another story.

Thinking back, much of what has come to pass in my wildlife conservation career I owe to a remarkable dog who brought three friends together at just the right time and in just the right place. Good old Kilo never returned to Ithaca to receive his college diploma. He "quit school" after his sophomore year and lived out the rest of a very good long life with my parents in Mastic Beach. In case you're wondering, he never ever grew tired of chasing those damn tennis balls.

LESSON LEARNED:

In my humble opinion, a dog's devotion to humans is unmatched in the animal kingdom. *Canis familiaris* fully deserves the title "Man's Best Friend." In my case, the friendship of a dog helped build lasting relationships with colleagues around the world.

MALE AFRICAN LION, KENYA, 2006

WE ARE NOT
CAT FOOD

Njalo elamini uya waletha   *Always, brother, you bring*
amathamsanqa, A-la-la-la, la-la.   *good fortune, A-la-la-la, la-la.*

Mbube.   *Mbube.*

Uyimbube.   *Uyimbube.*

Solomon Linda, "Mbube" (1939), translated from Zulu
(the original "The Lion Sleeps Tonight")

"**Young** man, do you have a moment?" The white-haired gentleman standing by the fireplace motioned to me as I was about to leave the room. Perhaps two strides shy of the door, I slowed and turned. I already had pulled the hood strings on my parka tight around my face to brace against the raw winter winds that can whip across Cayuga Lake, the longest of Upstate New York's glacial Finger Lakes. The request didn't come from just anyone. The man who asked if I had "a moment" was none other than world-renowned paleoanthropologist Dr. Louis Leakey. A moment? I had as many moments as Dr. Leakey needed. He was visiting Cornell as a professor-at-large, an honorary title that carried the obligation to lecture occasionally on campus. Dr. Leakey had just given an hour of his Saturday morning to students in my physical anthropology class, regaling us with stories of his fossil-hunting expeditions in Africa.

"Might you be able to spare a few hours of your time this weekend to assist me? I'm working on a special project and am in need of some reference materials for my presentation. It would be wonderful to have a little help from someone familiar with the campus, someone who may be able to fetch a few papers and library texts. Would you have any interest in such a task?"

Was the man kidding? I was dumbstruck by the invitation. I seem to have this inexplicable knack for being in the right place at the right time. In this case, I confess that I was purposely dawdling to get one last look at the young woman who had accompanied Dr. Leakey on his visit to Ithaca. She was nothing short of a knockout—long brown hair flowing down to the small of her back (not that I remember every detail, but I remember every detail). She had walked through the room a couple of times during his storytelling, bringing in a few logs from the porch and loading them onto the wood rack next to the fireplace. The brief delay in my departure was perfectly timed.

In 1951, the year before I was born, Louis Leakey and his wife, Mary, began their fossil-hunting efforts in Tanzania's (then Tanganyika's) Olduvai Gorge. Eight years later, they discovered the bones of what became known as "Nutcracker Man"—a robust early relative of *Homo sapiens* who boasts the largest and strongest molar teeth of any known human ancestor.

Perhaps though, Dr. Leakey remembered my response to a question he'd asked a half hour earlier. He had been speaking about his Kenyan childhood and began to fumble in search of a word. He couldn't remember the name of a small African hunting dog that doesn't bark. I had just read about the breed, but sat silent, expecting that Dr. Leakey would eventually recall its name. When he didn't, and when no one else responded, I sheepishly blurted out, "Do you mean the basenji?" I had never been to Africa and had not laid eyes on the creature, but my response made me appear knowledgeable, singling me out from the other students. Dr. Leakey's smile and the nod of his head would have been reward enough for the experience, but I sure as hell wasn't going to turn down the offer to be his library gopher.

I turned from the door and re-entered the room, took off my parka and set it on a chair by the door. The alluring young woman was stacking the last of the logs next to the fireplace. Dr. Leakey gestured for me to take a seat on the couch so we might discuss logistics. "As I mentioned," he explained, "I'll be in need of someone to help with some last-minute research I'm doing in preparation for a presentation in Washington, DC. I'll be making a report to the National Geographic Society and showing some slides of recent fieldwork. I'd appreciate someone else's opinion regarding the images I've chosen since Cindy here has seen many of them already." The young woman who had been kneeling as she adjusted the stack of logs, stood and smiled at the mention of her name. "Oh, please allow me to introduce my young traveling companion from California who, unfortunately, doesn't know a soul here in town. I think Cindy very well might appreciate having an escort this weekend and to my upcoming lecture. Might that be possible as well?"

This is exactly the point where you wake up and realize that all the events that have just transpired are merely a dream. But they weren't and I could see that Dr. Leakey was expecting a reply. I was finding it just a bit difficult to contain my enthusiasm, which threatened to erupt as a leap into the air, right arm extended upwards with a resounding "Yes!" Thankfully, Dr. Leakey interjected before I could embarrass myself. "Oh, please forgive me, young man, I neglected to ask your name."

"I'm Bill. Bill Konstant," I answered, reaching to shake his hand as well as Cindy's, who had moved from the fireplace to join the conversation. I learned that she was an undergraduate student at UCLA and was accompanying the eminent paleontologist on his trip east. It seemed that a rugby injury from Dr. Leakey's youth had returned to haunt him, and his 69-year-old bones were a bit unsteady. So, in addition to helping one of the world's most famous paleontologists, he was asking me to spend a couple of days escorting this young woman around town. What's the expression? Oh, yeah, "It's a tough job, but somebody's gotta do it."

My part-time job at Cornell's Mann Library provided me easy access to all of the references that Dr. Leakey required. He was preparing two talks: one for his sponsors at the National Geographic Society and another for our student and faculty audience. This was back in the days of Kodak Carousel projectors, so the three of us spent a fair amount of time that weekend shuffling and reshuffling trays of 35mm slides. The image of a warthog urinating outside its burrow elicited a chuckle from Dr. Leakey, "And here we have a female warthog spending a penny." The phrase, he explained, came from the history of public toilet use in Great Britain. Apparently, men's toilets were available free of charge, while women had to deposit one pence for the privilege of their use. "You know," he remarked, "warthogs are incredibly interesting animals, but no one has yet taken on the task of studying them. I think their behavior would make for a very rewarding research subject. What are your thoughts regarding that?"

I pondered the implicit suggestion. As a college sophomore who had just started shaving a year earlier, this world-renowned scientist was tempting me to consider an opportunity that could potentially come complete with its own career path. Was Louis Leakey—the man who had sent Jane Goodall to Gombe to study chimpanzees and Dian Fossey to Rwanda to study mountain gorillas—hinting that I consider going to Africa to study warthogs? Or was he just asking if I shared his particular fascination with this species? I tilted my head in contemplation, "Maybe a research project for graduate school?" That was the best I could muster on short notice. We returned to sorting slides. That evening, as a reward, I was treated to a home-

SERENGETI NATIONAL PARK, TANZANIA, 2007

cooked meal prepared by one of the world's most distinguished anthropologists, including a couple of hefty slices of his famous "Leakey bread." It was his family recipe—the very recipe used when the Leakeys gathered around the cooking fire in the Olduvai Gorge after a day of digging fossils.

The following evening, more than a thousand people filled Bailey Hall to attend Dr. Leakey's lecture: "Man's Fossil Ancestors and Near Cousins." His talk focused on early humans and the other mammals—both predators and prey—that coevolved on the African savannas. He emphasized that our ancestors were scavengers as well as hunters. He also contended that lions and leopards may not have been a major threat to our predecessors, and that—in his opinion—big cats were not particularly fond of human flesh. He remarked, "I don't know why, but emphatically, we are not cat food." I took that to mean that early man evolved in an environment in which there was no shortage of prey for large predators like African lions and leopards.

Dr. Leakey returned to England shortly after his visit across the pond. Several months later, still 69 years old, he passed from a heart attack.

MALE LIONS MAKE THEIR WAY ACROSS THE NGORONGORO CRATER, TANZANIA, 2005

It was a privilege crossing this great man's path. Our conversations had me thinking more and more about lions, leopards and other big cats, and that would one day lead me to Africa.

It would take more than 20 years to see my first wild lions in Africa. I was leading a tourist safari to Tanzania while employed by the Houston Zoo. Our group spent two days in the Ngorongoro Crater, one of the most incredible wildlife displays on our planet. The volcanic crater is home to thriving populations of lions, elephants, zebra, giraffe, buffalo, wildebeests, rhinos and many other spectacular creatures. Half a million people visit each year. Our vehicle was among a dozen or more lazily making their way through the middle of the crater, following faint traces of dusty roads in an immense open landscape.

Off in the distance, our driver spotted two large black-maned lions, regal felines with magnificent coiffures that must have been the envy of all the other resident lions. Like us, the likely brothers were in no hurry. This meant that all the drivers in

LIONESSES, SOUTH AFRICA, 2002

the vicinity had plenty of time to jockey for positions that would offer their passengers the best possible view of the duo. A throng of Land Rovers and Land Cruisers lurched closer to the approaching big cats, some vehicles abandoning the dirt road and venturing into the low grass to close the gap. Several passengers in our car simultaneously volunteered their advice to the driver. "Get us over there!" I noticed that each was pointing in a different direction. The driver glanced at me for a little help.

"How about, instead of moving forward, we turn away from all the other cars?" I suggested.

My companions all shook their heads, clearly thinking, "Why in blazes should we move away from the approaching lions?"

"How about we turn around?" I looked out the back window at the perfect spot. "We can park ourselves right over there, right in the middle of the crater." I pointed to where the two dirt tracks crossed—the same area that all the other cars had abandoned as they headed to "new and better" vantage points.

My companions remained unconvinced, still shaking their heads and now grumbling.

"Here's what I think is going to happen," I offered. "Very soon, those two bad boys are going to shift course. I think they'll decide to avoid the crowds and walk along the dirt road instead. In fact, if we park right there in the crossroad, I'm betting they'll walk right past us." Our driver smiled in agreement, nodded and restarted the engine. My travel mates kept pointing at the other vehicles.

The next couple of minutes were very long ones, but, almost imperceptibly, the two big cats began to veer away from the throng of vehicles before them and move toward ours. The guy sitting next to me exclaimed, "Would you look at that!" Everyone grabbed their cameras, pointed their telephoto lenses out the open windows and focused on the lions, which were now walking straight toward us.

"Okay, all hands, arms and cameras inside the vehicle!" I commanded. "You can balance your lenses on the window frames, but I don't want to see any appendages, hats, camera straps or anything else anywhere near the lions when they pass us."

Just as predicted, the pair had shifted their course. It took all of one minute for two of the most impressive lions I have ever seen to stroll right beside us, their thick black manes literally within arm's reach. Trying to touch them, of course, was verboten. You can just imagine the dinner conversation.

"Can you believe it?? I actually touched a lion!"

We would naturally have had to refer to that person as "Lefty" for the rest of the trip and probably wouldn't have been able to retrieve his or her missing limb. And, now that I'm thinking of

YOUNG MALE LION WITH ZEBRA KILL, SERENGETI NATIONAL PARK, TANZANIA, 2005

it, we would have proved that, in certain cases, we *are* cat food along with zebra, warthogs, wildebeest, impala, gazelles and a host of other prey species.

I've spent time with lions in Tanzania, Kenya and South Africa, both in the company of tourists and conservation colleagues. Unfortunately, although it is still easy to observe wild prides in a number of national parks and nature reserves, Africa's lions are disappearing across the continent and their populations are in steep decline. Expanding human populations significantly reduce lion habitat and the availability of the big cat's prey. As lions are forced into closer contact with people, the predators kill cattle and goats when unable to find antelope and buffalo. People then retaliate by shooting or poisoning the lions. Poachers kill lions for their meat and bones, which are popular items in Asian medicine, much the same as rhinoceros horn. Heavy wire snares intended for other wildlife also injure lions often leading to painful deaths.

The largest remaining lion populations—between 1,000 and 4,000 cats—are in East Africa. They live in protected areas such as the Selous Game Reserve, Ruaha National Park and the Serengeti. Southern Africa is home to lion populations of 2,000 or more in areas such as the Okavango Delta and the Greater Limpopo Transfrontier Park. Combined, the above regions probably hold three-quarters of all lions remaining on the African continent.

They also are home to critical conservation initiatives such as the Niassa Carnivore Project in Mozambique (one of several Lion Guardians' projects across the continent), Tanzania's African People and Wildlife and the Ruaha Carnivore Project, Ewaso Lions in Kenya, and the Botswana Predator Conservation Trust.

All of these endeavors enlist the help of local communities to protect these magnificent beasts; they also benefit other threatened carnivores such as leopards, hyenas, cheetahs and African wild dogs.

LESSON LEARNED:
Whenever opportunities arise, it's important to engage experienced individuals who are willing to impart wisdom, share their stories and perhaps dangle possibilities that will tempt your career-oriented passions. For the budding animal behaviorist, as I was back in the day, it's important to study your subjects with great care, so that when novel situations arise you will stand a halfway decent chance of predicting the outcomes.

LIONESS AND CUB EYE A GROUP OF GRAZING BUFFALOES
MASAI MARA NATIONAL RESERVE IN KENYA, 2006

HOW I EARNED THE NICKNAME "WRESTLES WITH WOLVES"

WRESTLES WITH
WOLVES

*For the strength of the wolf is the pack
and the strength of the pack is the wolf.*

Rudyard Kipling
"Law for the Wolves," *The Jungle Book* (1894)

"Would you like to meet our wolves?" Neda didn't have to ask me twice. Of course, I wanted to meet her wolves.

Neda was one of my wife Nannette's quilting buddies. For many years, she and her husband, Bob, had bred dogs, mainly Doberman pinschers and Rottweilers, but they also had a small pack of timber wolves on their Pennsylvania farm. You don't come across that all too often just a stone's throw from a big city.

She had no way of knowing that I was a Mowgli wannabe, a *Jungle Book* junkie. I firmly believe that I, too, would have survived life in the jungle had I been raised by wolves. I seem to have a way with animals, not only with pets but wild creatures as well. Over the years, some have called me a "whisperer," though I'm not sure there really is such a thing. I can't speak the languages of the beasts like Doctor Dolittle. I have never imagined myself swinging from a jungle vine like Tarzan. And there's zero chance that I'll ever try to grab a tiger snake, taipan or death adder by the tail like the late Steve Irwin. However, for as long as I can remember, I've felt a special connection to fellow beings—an ability to sense an animal's mood, to know when it's safe to approach, as well as to realize when I might be in danger.

But for now, I had wolves on my mind. Neda pointed the way, "Just walk down the hill until you see Bob's red pick-up. It's probably parked by the wolf pen. He should be feeding them their morning meal."

The red pick-up was parked on the side of a dirt road under the summer shade of a large oak tree. Bob was nowhere to be seen, but the driver's side door was wide open, so I walked over and looked inside. A humongous, square-faced dog sat in the passenger's seat. Drool dripped from her lower lip as she sat staring, laser-focused on me. The dog looked like a mastiff of some sort and probably weighed as much as I did with a head as big as a bowling ball. She continued to stare as I closed the distance between us, ultimately crossing the invisible line that could initiate a flight or fight response. In this case, there was no route to retreat. The passenger-side door was shut behind the mastiff, so flight was not an option.

"Hey, pup!" That's how I greet any new dog. I offered the back of my hand, palm down, and let the dog sniff away. Having been bitten by a couple of neighborhood dogs—a boxer and a German shepherd—when I was a young boy, I know the consequences of misreading the signs, of miscalculating the dog's next move. I carefully watched the mastiff's facial expression for any sign that she might be thinking "Okay, clown, you're going to regret this *big-time*!" As I swung in behind the steering wheel and grabbed it with my left hand, the dog sniffed up and down my right arm and apparently detected no threat. I slowly retracted my right arm, grabbed the other side of the steering wheel and looked straight ahead, basically ignoring my host. Her next move was to lean in closer and sniff my hair. Had I misjudged the dog's mood, this was where I would pay the price. It would be the perfect opportunity for her to bite off my ear. Instead, she nuzzled closer, which I took as an invitation to scratch behind *her* ears.

CINNAMON AND ERIC, KIMBERTON, PA, 2003

It was at that point that Bob emerged from a small building up ahead, a storehouse that adjoined the wolf pen. A bucket of chicken parts in one hand, he closed the door behind him, turned in our direction and looked up to see me sitting in his truck, befriending his big pooch. He nearly dropped the bucket.

"Bill?"

"Yeah! Hi, Bob!"

Bob grinned and shook his head. Had his hands not been otherwise occupied, I think he would have rubbed his eyes and looked again to make sure they weren't deceiving him. "Neda said you were coming down to see our wolves, but she didn't tell me you were crazy!"

"What do you mean?" The dog continued to lean against me and I kept scratching her behind the ears.

"Cinnamon has never let anyone but me sit with her in that truck! I'm surprised she let you within 10 yards of it!"

"Dogs just love me, I guess!"

Cinnamon the guard dog and I were much more alike than we were different, and I somehow sensed that she bore me no malice. Bob walked up to the open truck door, put down the bucket, took off his gloves, and we shook hands. I had saved him the

ERIC THE TIMBER WOLF, KIMBERTON, PA, 2003

trouble of introducing me to such a ferocious beast. Bob explained that Cinnamon was a *Fila Brasileira*, a Brazilian mastiff. I had heard of the breed but had never met one before. It is not at all common here in the United States and is best known for protecting cattle against jaguars and other predators in South American rain forests and savannas.

Here on a Pennsylvania farm, with no jaguars to worry about, Cinnamon protected Bob, Neda, their kennel dogs and their wolves. She even helped them raise one of the wolf pups. A year earlier, one of the wolves became gravely sick and could not take care of her baby. Bob and Neda stepped in, Cinnamon stepped up and Eric, the wolf pup, was now as big as an adult.

Cinnamon jumped out of the truck to chaperone Bob and me on our walk to Eric's pen. Bob unlocked and unlatched the gate, and Eric trotted out to join us. But before the young wolf could greet us humans, he was obliged to acknowledge his surrogate mom. Cinnamon stood stiff-legged in front of us, head held tall and straight. Eric was taller, but his frame shrunk below hers and his head dipped below her jaws. Cinnamon curled her upper lip and growled. The young wolf whined faintly and licked the mastiff's chin. I sensed her message to him: "You behave yourself now! This crazy human thinks he's one of us. Don't forget who the real boss is around here!" Cinnamon's insight was impressive.

ERIC MEETS THE NEIGHBOR'S COWS, KIMBERTON, PENNSYLVANIA, 2003

With the formal introductions completed, Bob handed me Eric's leash. The young wolf readily accepted me as a member of his pack thanks to a bond forged thousands of years ago between our two species. To this day, scientists debate the origins and evolutionary path of this relationship. Suffice it to say, over countless generations, humans and this apex canine predator developed a mutually beneficial relationship that transcends cultures and gives us the incredible variety of dog breeds we enjoy today.

The young wolf and I spent the next hour or so walking the property's hills and woodlands, and splashing in the creek. He never once resisted my lead, tested the leash or attempted to run away. At one point, Eric and I climbed a small hill that brought us to the boundary with a neighbor's farm. A small herd of cows stood in the field beyond, grazing on the tall grass. The wire fence between us was barely visible. With a leap and a few short bounds, Eric could have easily cleared the fence and sunk his teeth into some prime sirloin. So how did he react? He turned tail and ran back behind me as far as the leash would allow. I joked

RICK MCINTYRE AND ANNIE GRAHAM, YELLOWSTONE NATIONAL PARK, 2004

with the big guy, laughing, "Why, you little coward!" I didn't know then that Eric had not seen cows before. It didn't take long for him to regain his composure and return to the fence, standing in front of me and staring at the cows. They hadn't budged, but I could see that Eric had gained their attention. He didn't lick his lips, but I imagined he could have been thinking, "Beef, it's what's for dinner!"

Before it came time for my new wolf friend to return to his pen, Bob let me take off Eric's leash so the two of us could "wrassle" a bit in the grass. I dropped on all fours and signaled with my hand for Eric to engage. He came in low, aiming for the opposite shoulder, letting me dip down, reach under his belly, latch on to a rear leg and go for the takedown. That put the wolf on his back and his tail in my face. It was probably good that I couldn't see his open mouth and teeth flashing at that point.

Eric and I rolled around in the grass. For a few magical minutes, I was Mowgli play-fighting with one of my wolf cub brothers or sisters.

A year after meeting Eric, I ran into a few of his wild relatives in Yellowstone National Park. A local rancher who supported research on the wolves that had been reintroduced to Yellowstone had invited me to attend a national conference about wolves. That rancher, Annie Graham, also funded a program with Defenders of Wildlife to compensate fellow ranchers who might have legitimate claims of livestock lost to wandering wolf packs. Late in the afternoon the day before the conference started, Annie and field biologist Rick McIntyre took me out into the National Park to meet the Druid Peak wolf pack.

Gathering clouds obscured a sinking sun as dusk approached. I stood near Soda Butte Cone in the Lamar Valley along with maybe a half-dozen other folks, our binoculars and spotting scopes trained on the nearby foothills. Rick lifted his right arm skyward, holding the H-shaped radio receiver antenna in the direction of Druid Peak, two miles to our northwest. He slowly swept the device back and forth in a small arc.

Blip. Blip. Blip. Rick was homing in on a transmitter attached to one of the radio-collared wolves in the Druid Peak pack. His receiver confirmed that the pack was close, probably just on the other side of the ridge. The next sound we heard was a long, low, plaintive howl—first one and then joined by another and another until the entire wolf pack was contributing to the chorus. The vibrations penetrated my flesh. Goosebumps rose on my arms. The sensation was primal, but not one of fear. The howling ended as quickly as it had begun. Incredible. I was hearing wild wolves for the first time in my life. Recordings made for movies and television documentaries pale by comparison.

Blip. Blip. Blip. Blip. We couldn't yet see the wolves, but the cadence and intensity of "blips" told us that they were moving in our direction. All eyes focused on the ridge top.

BLIP. BLIP. BLIP. BLIP. BLIP. The lead wolf cleared the ridge without breaking stride, followed by the rest of the pack. They were not in any hurry and they didn't seem to notice what remained of a two-day-old elk kill in the flats.

I was witnessing the return of an endangered species, one that had given rise to "man's best friend" yet had been ruthlessly slaughtered by man—hunted down, trapped and poisoned for more than a century. And that was before I was even born. The gray or timber wolf (they're one and the same), one of the most dominant predators in North America, was almost entirely eradicated from the lower 48 states. Wolves had called Yellowstone home for millennia, but cattle and sheep ranchers and bounty hunters had done them in by the early 1900s. Thanks to the Endangered Species Act, wildlife biologists were able to reintroduce wolves to the National Park in 1995. The Druid Peak pack—the wolves we were observing that evening— was evidence of the project's success.

The wolves passed in single file. They were less than a hundred yards from our group. They wound their way between us and a small herd of bison about the same distance to their other side. The herd seemed less interested in the pack than we were. The American bison, which many know better as "buffalo," has also called the Yellowstone area home for millennia. It has forever been an important food source for the timber wolf.

Bison are not

buffalo. Buffalo are native to Asia and Africa. Bison are native to Europe and North America. So the next time you sing the iconic American song "Home on the Range" and get to the part "... where the buffalo roam ..." substitute "bison" for "buffalo."

For thousands of years, Native Americans also relied on bison for survival. They found uses for just about every inch of the animal,

BISON STOPPING TRAFFIC, YELLOWSTONE NATIONAL PARK, 2014

carving knives, awls, scrapers and pipes from the bones. Hides were fashioned into robes, tipi coverings, moccasins and quivers. Bison hair could be woven into ropes and bracelets or used to stuff pillows and dolls. And horns were excellent for holding gunpowder or for crafting cups, spoons and ladles.

I had an up-close-and-personal encounter with a bison cow some years before, during my zookeeper days at the Long Island Game Farm. Her name was Calamity Jane and she was getting ready to drop her first calf. Daddy was a bull bison named Buffalo Bill. I was assigned to assist Dr. John Andresen, the zoo's veterinarian, with the delivery, which seemed to be stalled. Jane was having some difficulty. John and I were standing outside the bison enclosure, leaning against the fence when he decided we needed to help.

"Bill, have you ever lassoed a bison?"

"No, John, can't say that I have. Why? Do you want me to try to lasso Jane?"

CALAMITY JANE AND ME, LONG ISLAND GAME FARM, 1970S

"I think it's a good option at this point. If you can get this rope over her horns, I'd like to see if we can pull her to the corner of the pen. Then, if we can get her calmed down just a bit, I'll be able to see what's holding things up. The calf may need to be turned and eased out."

I had never tried my hand at lassoing before, but I couldn't think of a good reason not to give it a shot. "Okay, let me have the rope."

John handed me the lasso (which was a lot heavier and stiffer than I imagined it would be). I looped it over my shoulder and hopped the fence. Upon seeing me enter the adjoining pen, Buffalo Bill left his morning meal half-finished and galloped over to the wood and wire barrier that separated us (and kept me from being gored and trampled). Earlier, I'd confided to John that I had been in the pen with Jane before, standing face-to-face with her while she allowed me to scratch the top of her head. She had never shown any aggression toward me, but bison-related injuries to zookeepers are not unheard of, so the risks of unprotected contact are very real indeed, especially when you're talking about an animal that might weigh close to a quarter of a ton. Since Jane had become used to me walking up to her, she wasn't intimidated as I moved in her direction. The rope was something new, however, so I didn't push my luck. I got as close as I could without spooking her and then stopped, holding the rope at my hip. She held her ground as well. One step more and she would either turn and run or charge me. In her condition, I was willing to bet she'd run.

Slowly, I raised my right arm, holding the lasso above my head, and began to make small circles with my wrist, which widened the loop. This didn't seem to faze her, so I let go of the rope, watched it fly toward her, then land squarely atop her head and hump. That let me pull the loop taut around the base of her horns. Instead of trying to pull a quarter-ton bison toward me, it seemed like a better idea just to walk my hands along the rope, maintaining minimal tension, and approach her the same way I had done on previous occasions. It took a little time, but Jane didn't bolt. In fact, she tolerated restraint with the rope and let John take up a position to her rear and begin the delivery. Elbow-deep into the procedure, he determined that the calf was breech; it was backward in the uterus so a little bit of muscle was needed to twist its body around for a head-first entrance into the world. Before you knew it, a mucous-covered, wobbly-legged baby bison struggled to stand and take his first steps. Perhaps his birth symbolized the struggle that his species had survived a century before.

Western expansion decimated America's vast bison herds. The slaughter was relentless; the carnage was nearly complete and, in the end, the United States government's campaign to clear

A BISON CALF AND ME, LONG ISLAND GAME FARM, 1970S
PHOTO COURTESY OF LONG ISLAND GAME FARM

the land of bison ultimately achieved its real goal of demoralizing and dominating the indigenous people of this land. Biologists estimate that, at its peak, North America's bison population may have numbered 50 million or more. By the end of the Civil War, probably only half that number remained. And, in a period of only 10 to 20 years, the entire species was almost exterminated. A million animals or more a year died. If my math is correct, for more than a decade an average of close to 2,800 bison bit the dust every day. That's more than 100 every hour or about two every single minute—for more than 10 years. We'll never again experience the seemingly endless, thundering herds of the American West.

There was a time that few thought we'd see wolves back in Yellowstone. Yet, here I was, watching the Druid Peak wolves—white, gray and black among them—striding past the grazing bison and showing little interest in the potential prey. I imagined the leader explaining to the rest of the pack, "We ate a big meal only a couple of days ago, so there's no reason to waste any time or energy on these cud-chewers. Let's just keep moving and find a good place over the next hill to bed down for the night." The bison stopped feeding momentarily as the wolves approached. Their breath condensed in snorts of vapor rising from their nostrils, quickly vanishing in the air above their horns. Somehow, they sensed that it wasn't dinner time, or at least that bison steaks weren't on the menu. One by one, the bison calmly resumed ruminating their dinner of grass while the wolves disappeared over the next rise and into the darkness.

The Yellowstone wolf restoration project actually had minimal impact on the species' survival overall. Today, the gray or timber wolf roams across more than 60 North American, European and Asian countries. It has disappeared from four: Ireland, Japan, the United Kingdom and possibly Bangladesh. The IUCN Red List of Threatened Species designates the wolf's conservation status as "Least Concern." That certainly doesn't mean that the return of wolves to Yellowstone was merely symbolic, especially if you consider how it has rebooted the local ecology.

The returning wolves began thinning large deer and elk populations. That led to a regeneration of meadows and increased tree growth, which means better habitat for songbirds and greater food production for wildlife in general, such as more berries for grizzlies and black bears. With the predators of olden days back in town and roaming the valleys, elk herds are on the move once more instead of lollygagging about browsing trees and bushes down to the nubs. Streamside vegetation is taking hold again and soil erosion has declined significantly. More and bigger trees along riverbanks provide building material for

ERIC AND ME WRESTLING, KIMBERTON, PENNSYLVANIA, 2003

ever-industrious beavers. Their numbers have grown along with their dams, increasing Yellowstone's wetland habitat for fish, amphibians and reptiles.

Returning wolves have been a boon to the local economy as well. Since 1995's reintroduction, Americans drive from across the country just to see "their wolves." They and tourists from around the world stay at local hotels and motels, eat at restaurants and hire outfitters who take them wildlife-watching. Farms and ranches help fuel this system. Family members who aren't tilling the soil or managing the herds often take jobs in the resurging industries driven by Yellowstone's once again thriving wildlife.

Yellowstone is the only place in the United States where the American bison never disappeared. They've called the area home since prehistoric times. The Park's herd is the largest on public land, numbering right around 5,000 bison—large enough to

create the occasional traffic jam. Nationwide, an estimated half million bison roam—a far cry from historic highs but a healthy population nonetheless.

LESSON LEARNED:

The combined experiences of wolf wrestling, bison birthing and witnessing the results of both species' survival in the wild have had an enormous impact on me. They made it clear that my childhood fascination with animals was also my passport to a very special world—a world in which I and others can help make a real difference in the efforts to save endangered species.

PANDORA, A CALIFORNIA SEA LION, DEMONSTRATING HER ACROBATIC TALENT, 1975
PHOTO COURTESY OF LONG ISLAND GAME FARM

NO PANDERING TO
PANDORA

I lived a season in the midst of a herd of them … They lay around me in every direction; they watched my fire and what I did … They scratch their ears and head with their hind flippers … the young bleat like sheep, and while I was among them it seemed to me as if I were playing shepherd …

Georg Wilhelm Steller, *De Bestiis Marinas* (1751)
W. Miller & J.E. Miller, trans, *The Beasts of the Sea* (2011)

My summers as a zookeeper at the Long Island Game Farm during college became a full-time job as an animal trainer after graduation. My furred and feathered charges were farmyard animals who happened to be part-time thespians: Professor Punch, a rabbit that played the piano; Miss Judy, a chicken that challenged the audience to a shell game; Gambol the Goat—he raised the American flag to the top of the schoolhouse steeple; and Petunia the Pig who used her snout to open the closet and fetch me a broom so I could sweep the Barnyard Theater stage at the close of the show. Pretty hokey, I'll admit, but for two seasons I was able to put my college studies in neurobiology and behavior to practical use and hone my animal training skills across a diverse group of species.

After two seasons of working with chickens, rabbits, goats and pigs (despite how fond of them I was), I welcomed the Game Farm's decision to revamp its performing animal attraction. The Barnyard Theater became the Sea School Theater and I became a sea lion trainer. The old red schoolhouse transformed into a wharf surrounded by an aqua sea with white-capped waves. The stage more than doubled in size and now sat right in front of a large kidney-shaped pool. The quaint wooden logs and benches for the audience were history. We now had a state-of-the-art concrete, steel and fiberglass amphitheater large enough to host as many as 500 people. I swapped my red-checkered shirt and blue jeans for surfer shorts and a captain's hat and became quite handy behind the scenes with a fish knife. How much a sea lion eats varies widely depending on where they live, how big they are, whether they have nursing babies and the list goes on. In fact, researchers have found that a lactating mom in the wild can eat almost a quarter of her body weight every day.

Seals, sea lions and walruses are pinnipeds—fin-footed marine mammals. Six species of sea lions still roam our planet, but the health of their populations varies widely from Least Concern to Endangered. Populations of California and South American sea lions are of Least Concern. The Steller sea lion is Near Threatened, while Australian, New Zealand and Galápagos sea lions are Endangered. Threats to wild populations include a lack of food from overfishing, residential and commercial development along coastal habitats and the impacts of climate change.

Since the 1970s, we've witnessed a bit of a baby boom off the West Coast. In 1972, the Marine Mammal Protection Act took effect, and it has helped the once-depleted wild populations of California sea lions rebound.

Speaking of California sea lions, I'll never forget the day that one named Pandora galumphed her way into my world. She was a Florida family's house pet. She had had free run of their home and property, and spent much of her day cruising the canal bordering their backyard. A rash of biting complaints lodged by neighbors ultimately rendered Pandora sea lion non grata. That, along with the fact that she could not fend for herself in the wild, sealed the deal for a one-way ticket from sunny Florida to snowy New York.

WILD SEA LIONS BASKING, THE ROCKS OFF THE COAST OF LA JOLLA, 2010

Pandora arrived at John F. Kennedy International Airport late one winter afternoon. An hour and a half later, a truck with Pandora on board pulled up to her new home in the middle of Long Island. It took four of us to unload her crate, hefting it just in front of her open holding pen. The door was opened so she could enter, but a sea lion-sized space left between the crate and pen gave Pandora room for a detour. She eased out of her crate about halfway, then quickly turned on her agile front flippers, shoved herself through the gap and barreled her way around the crate in my direction. In a split second, my new sea lion partner's muzzle was wedged firmly against my crotch, pinning me up against her pen. I took a deep breath and vividly remember watching her long whiskers flick back and forth as she breathed heavily and sniffed my groin. Fortunately, Pandora decided to leave my manhood intact. Instead, she inched back of her own volition and waddled forward into her holding pen.

Pandora and I embarked on daily training sessions. I felt confident that they would provide her the enrichment she required and a positive outlet for interacting with people. I gave Pandora the time she needed to adjust to her new surroundings, allowing her ample free time in the big pool to acclimate to the New York winter. Then I introduced her to a wooden platform. Her eyes focused on her target: the tennis ball-on-a-stick in my left hand. She hoisted herself onto her assigned seat. I dipped my right hand into the small bucket of fish strapped at my waist and offered her a six-inch smelt as a reward, but just not quickly enough to avoid what happened next.

PANDORA "PORPOISES" FOR A MIDDAY CROWD, 1975
PHOTO COURTESY OF LONG ISLAND GAME FARM

Pandora rocketed off the platform straight at me. I was stunned and had no time to react as she rammed her open mouth into my thigh. That knocked me backward, feet in the air, as she blasted past me and splashed into the pool. I was fortunate. The double layer of clothing I was wearing—workman's coveralls over blue jeans— didn't cushion the blow all that much, but the extra padding did spare my skin from being broken. I suffered only a six-inch-wide, deep-purple bruise to my leg, not to mention the bruise to my ego.

There was really no way to employ positive reinforcement in this situation—essentially rewarding Pandora for not hurting her trainer more seriously—so I focused on conveying to her that I was pissed (maybe more at myself than at her). I needed to make clear that such behavior was simply unacceptable. I picked up a baton and shook it above my head, glaring at her in the pool and bringing the training session to an abrupt end. Then I opened the gate to her pen and backed away, allowing her to retreat to safety. That gave her a time-out. Since it was nearly lunchtime, I used that to my advantage. I let Pandora stew for a few minutes while I prepared half her daily ration of fish. I carried her bowl of fish along with my own lunch—a tuna sandwich—to her pen, opened the gate and walked in.

Pandora moved to the far end, allowing me to sit down at the edge of the wooden pallet that kept her body off the bare concrete. I placed the bowl of fish beside me, took my sandwich from the brown paper bag and began to munch away. Pandora just sat and stared at me as I ate. Then, very slowly and deliberately, she inched her left front flipper in my direction. I clicked my cricket (the name given to the dime store clickers that animal trainers used back in the day) and tossed a piece of fish from the bowl in her direction. Pandora scarfed it down, unblinking. Then she slowly swung her right front flipper around. *Click! Click!* I tossed her another piece of fish, which went down as quickly and easily as the first. Gradually, I coaxed my new friend closer and closer, and faster than you could say "Jack Robinson," there she was stretched across my legs with her snout buried in the bowl of fish beside me. She received her final reward that session for just sniffing—not biting—my hand when I offered a smelt to her.

Pandora came to accept me unconditionally. We became "interspecific companions"—buddies, for short. She, however, a perennial problem for the other trainers, threatening them every so often and catching them off guard; they never lost their fear of her biting them. My advice was pretty

PANDORA AND I TAKE A BREAK TOGETHER TO READ THE DAYS NEWS, 1975
PHOTO COURTESY OF LONG ISLAND GAME FARM

straightforward: "If you don't sit down and have lunch with that 'bad girl,' she'll never fully accept you." My colleagues didn't buy it and I certainly understood their reluctance. The show went on, despite Pandora occasionally snapping at the other trainers. She was an excellent performer, intelligent and quick to learn.

In fact, learning something new in itself was a very powerful reward for Pandora. An all-time favorite for the audience was when she'd leap into the pool, torpedo to the front wall, and whip her flipper back and forth, showering the people in the first few rows with waves of water. My personal favorite was when she and I pretended to argue with one another. We'd go head-to-head, our faces only inches apart, her mouth wide open, teeth bared with the smell of fish assaulting my nostrils. Pandora would roar straight into my microphone; the audience most likely believed that I was nuts. Then, when it looked as though the sea lion was going to rip off her trainer's face, I'd quickly turn my head and present my cheek—Pandora's cue to snap her mouth shut and plant a wet, sloppy kiss just above my chin. None of the other trainers ever tried this stunt, and I'm pretty sure it had nothing to do with Pandora's fishy breath.

The Game Farm received a fair number of applicants who wanted to work with sea lions, among them a young blond-haired woman by the name of Lisa de Kooning. The only child of Willem de Kooning, the famed Dutch-born abstract expressionist artist, Lisa had a passion for working with animals and was more than willing to make the 40-mile drive to work from her family home in the Hamptons. What I remember most about her interview was the mention of typical household guests. She casually dropped the name of the legendary Sir Paul McCartney. Being a friend or an acquaintance of one of the Beatles certainly raised the point score on her application. Despite that, I wound up not hiring Lisa, giving the job instead to a local young woman, a somewhat less illustrious but equally earnest candidate.

Since my days with Pandora, I've visited other zoos and aquariums that feature sea lion encounters. For a hunk of mackerel, Rocky, a big bull sea lion and a crowd favorite at the Houston Zoo, was more than happy to smack a sloppy kiss on the face of any consenting guest. Even the most tentative recipients couldn't resist and would come under Rocky's spell, smiling the broadest and toothiest grins you could imagine. The Houston Zoo calls its sea lions "ambassadors for marine conservation initiatives" in the United States and abroad—initiatives that help protect species that include sea turtles and the endangered Galápagos sea lion.

ROCKY, A CALIFORNIA SEA LION, PLANTS A "WET ONE" ON VISITING CINCINNATI ZOO
DIRECTOR THANE MAYNARD, THE HOUSTON ZOO, 2004

One Saturday evening, after a full day of sea lion shows before packed crowds, I returned home and headed straight to the bathroom for a long hot shower, hoping to wash away the aroma of mackerel that had permeated my clothes and clung to my skin. Afterward, I sat on the living room couch to read a magazine article or two while Nan prepared our dinner. At the time, she and I were renting a small bungalow from my aunt and uncle, a cozy residence in our hometown of Mastic Beach on the south shore of Long Island. A white picket fence ran along the street front and we had a big backyard. I had just finished reading the feature article of *FOCUS*, the quarterly membership newsletter of the World Wildlife Fund. Its front page featured a young, shaggy-haired biologist holding a much younger, shaggy-haired orphaned orangutan. The photo was from a sanctuary that now had the task of raising the baby. Authorities had rescued him from the illegal pet trade. Most likely, poachers had killed the infant's mother to then sell him. For the next few years, the sanctuary would hand-raise the youngster in the company of other orphans with hopes of someday returning them to the wild in protected forest habitats.

I held the paper over my head in one hand and shook it, as if Nan could see it through the wall. "Hey, Punkin, this guy's got the best job in the world!"

"What guy?" The cottage was so small that we could have sat at opposite ends and carried on a conversation without raising our voices. In this case, had there been a small hole in the wall, she could have peeked over my shoulder and read the article herself.

"His name is Russ Mittermeier. He's a primate expert who works for the World Wildlife Fund. Says here that he went to Harvard, studied monkeys in the Amazon, and now he runs projects all over the world. Looks like he's only a few years older than us. Damn, what a great job! I'd love to work with this guy."

"Keep dreaming!" Nan's tone wasn't sarcastic or discouraging. She was just being realistic. We were still living where we had grown up. She had finished nursing school, secured a good job at a local hospital and seemed content pursuing her chosen career. I'd moved up the ladder from a summer zookeeper job to head sea lion trainer at the local zoo and was being considered for an assistant director's position. We had nothing to complain about, but reading the article made me think more seriously about what opportunities there might be to work in international wildlife conservation. My original major at Cornell was wildlife conservation, but I quickly switched to straight biology when I discovered that the wildlife conservation curriculum focused heavily on game management—as in controlling the hunting of deer, bear, rabbits, turkeys, pheasants and the like. I had zero interest in that. My hope of one day working to help save endangered species was still smoldering.

"Yeah, you're right, keep dreaming." I lowered the newsletter, placed it on the coffee table and continued to stare at the dude holding the orangutan. "By the way, what are we having for dinner?"

"Fish and chips!"

"As long as it's not mackerel!"

LESSON LEARNED:
Nan's simple advice to me was critical to guiding my journey: "Keep dreaming!" There's absolutely nothing wrong with dreaming. You know, I guess I'm not quite done with this chapter after all …

In 1494, on his second voyage to the New World, Columbus anchored his ship off Hispaniola's rocky southern coast. Several seamen went ashore, where they found then killed eight "sea wolves" that were basking on the beach. Such was the first encounter between Europeans and the Caribbean monk seal. At the time, the species was both widespread and abundant throughout the islands and the adjoining Gulf of Mexico. In the centuries that followed, however, the species was hunted relentlessly. Its blubber became lamp oil. Its food became scarce because of overfishing. The last confirmed sighting of a Caribbean monk seal was off the northern coast of Colombia in 1952, the year I was born. The IUCN declared the species Extinct in 2008. Two close relatives, the Hawaiian and Mediterranean monk seals, are both Endangered.

MONK SEAL BASKING ON WAIKIKI BEACH, OAHU, HAWAII, 2016

I'm now living my dream. As an advisor to the Mohamed bin Zayed Species Conservation Fund, I have had the opportunity to help my colleagues, who are hard at work saving threatened species, by approving grants to safeguard both seal species and their marine habitats.

WHITE-HANDED GIBBON, THE COLUMBUS ZOO, OHIO, 1985

TIME FOR SOME
MONKEY BUSINESS

It must be tough for a baboon to be asked by the other monkeys,
'What happened? Why do you have an airbag for a butt?'

Robin Williams
Inside the Actors Studio (2001)

Both Nan and I have relied on a healthy sense of humor to get us through the occasional tough stretch, but sometimes it just feels like life hits you with a knockout punch. Like there's no getting up. A family tragedy, which I'll share with you a bit later, left me no choice but to take a break from animal training while Nan took a leave of absence from nursing.

The wide-open road beckoned. We loaded a cargo carrier on the roof of our Ford Pinto hatchback. (Spoiler alert: the model known for exploding into flames did not provide such drama on our road trip.) We secured our 10-speed bikes to a rack on the rear. At 11 o'clock the night before we planned to hit the road, the head of the Pinto's engine was literally on the garage floor while Nan's auto mechanic brother, Paul, finished up the valve job he said the car needed before we drove west with no predetermined destination.

For six weeks, we sought solace and communed with Mother Nature, alternating between a tent and inexpensive hotels. The first night we set up camp under the shade and safety of a giant rhododendron in the Great Smoky Mountains, which essentially offered no protection during the surprise midnight rainstorm that flooded our tent and sleeping bags. Three weeks and three thousand miles later, we found ourselves in California's Sierra Nevada Mountains. We pitched our tent at a campground in Yosemite National Park. At dusk, standing beneath a canopy of giant sequoias reaching more than 200 feet into the sky, we gazed at the moon. As we scanned the heavens, we almost missed seeing a ghostly great gray owl that silently soared past us—no more than a foot above our heads—no doubt in search of some small unsuspecting rodent.

After returning to New York, Nan went back to work at Brookhaven Hospital. And I decided to try my hand at something entirely new: helping my dad start a small landscaping business. It was decent money, earned by honest days of hard work at the mercy of the elements. Breathing in the fresh salt air that blew across Long Island's famous East End beaches was a bonus.

After a couple of seasons into my newfound profession, however, I was distracted by an interesting help-wanted ad in the local newspaper. The State University of New York was looking for a "Primate Technician" at its Stony Brook campus. The "Primate" portion of the position caught my eye, but "Technician" significantly lessened the job's initial appeal. Animal behavior experience was required, so I thought it might be right up my alley. At the same time, I found myself fighting off images of monkeys with shaved heads and stitched-up incisions, cowering in the corners of stainless steel laboratory cages, but I decided to submit an application. The job turned out to be *not at all* what I had feared and the interview certainly not what I had expected.

Two Stony Brook professors, Dr. Jack Stern and Dr. Randall Susman, were co-investigators on a National Science Foundation grant for research that explored the mysteries of human origins. Their investigation focused on the behavior of monkeys and apes. The research premise was simple: Muscles, which all vertebrates rely on to move, are attached to bones at easily recognized points on the skeleton, so the functional

HORACE THE LORIS, STONY BROOK UNIVERSITY, NEW YORK, 1981

anatomy of living species can be compared, apples to apples, to the fossils of their ancestors. By examining the muscle activity of living primates during their everyday activities such as walking, running, jumping, climbing and swinging by their arms, Stern, Susman and their colleagues were able to compare physical features and gain insights into the likely behaviors of extinct species. They sought a better understanding of how humankind evolved. At what point did pre-humans begin to walk upright? Which fossil species might be considered "missing links" between modern-day men and women and our early primate cousins?

To conduct their research, the professors maintained a small colony of lemurs, lorises, spider monkeys, gibbons and chimpanzees. They needed a technician/trainer to ensure that these animals were physically sound, capable of a full range of normal activities and able to perform any of the desired

GIBBY THE MALE WHITE-HANDED GIBBON, STONY BROOK UNIVERSITY, NEW YORK, 1981

behaviors on command. They needed to behave as their wild relatives would. My job, should I be hired as a "personal trainer to the primates," was to ensure all of the above. There was only one problem: I wasn't a woman.

A female technician/trainer was leaving the project, which was why the position opened in the first place. She had done an excellent job with all the animals, but especially with a male white-handed gibbon by the name of Gibby. As it turns out, Gibby apparently loved women and hated men. It wasn't only that he wouldn't behave for a male trainer, he had bitten, scratched and tried to tear apart any person bearing a Y chromosome who dared enter his domain. Dr. Susman showed me a shirt that Gibby had effectively torn to shreds during one such incident.

My potential employers were impressed by my credentials, but also reluctant to offer me the job outright, so we reached a compromise. I suggested that I try training the notorious Gibby remotely, without having to enter his enclosure or be otherwise unprotected when within his reach. I was willing to guarantee his full cooperation during the experimental sessions without jeopardizing his safety, my safety or theirs. Fair enough. I was given a month to accomplish the goal or they'd find someone else.

Things actually started off pretty well between Gibby and me. He quickly abandoned attempts to grab me through the chain-link. I spent time watching him move about the large enclosure, then devised a set of verbal and hand commands that I would use to prompt various behaviors. As he completed each one and heard the sound of my trusty clicker, we developed a routine. He learned to approach me, extend his arm through the chain-link and accept a reward from my hand. Grapes and raisins were his favorite treats. Then, of course, the day came when he suckered me into coming a bit too close, shot his hand out past mine and tried to rip me a new face. Were there no barrier between us, he probably would have succeeded. My goal was to show Gibby that I was not a threat. He and I clearly needed to sort things out.

The next day, I gave him some alone time before we started, a chance to let our respective testosterone levels settle down. Then I picked up a push broom, let myself into the enclosure and closed the door behind me. I began to sweep the sawdust on the floor. Gibby watched from his perch on a branch high in the far corner. He hooted softly. That told me he was nervous and contemplating his next move. I knew what was coming and tightened my grip on the broom handle. In a flash, Gibby rocketed down on me like a heat-seeking missile, affording me just enough time to raise the business end of the broom. The bristles caught him square in the chops, bringing him to a dead

WHITE-HANDED GIBBONS, THE COLUMBUS ZOO, OHIO, 1985

stop midair. He dropped to the floor unhurt, even landing on his feet. Stunned but not shaken, he shook his head, spun around, ran back to the corner and swung himself up again to the highest branch. Round one to the trainer, but the bout was far from over. A second and a third ... umm ... "delicate dance" followed in rapid succession, each one thwarted by the broom bristles and followed by his retreat. The first session of Gibby's new training regimen concluded. I left the enclosure, gave him the rest of the day off and went to the hardware store to buy a new push broom.

The old broom had graduated from a cleaning implement and needed to be customized for its new job. Each day, I trimmed off a couple of inches of bristles, as well as about three or four inches of handle. I doubt that Gibby noticed the difference since I was still able to raise the smaller, shorter broom quickly enough in my defense each time he lunged. A gibbon's attack, coming from above, can be unnerving. Humans are programmed to deal best with adversaries that approach at ground level—not from the sky.

The interval between Gibby's and my tangos began to lengthen and their intensity lessened. In between, I made sure to reinforce his good behavior by tossing him a grape when he let me step in his direction. In a couple of weeks—well within my probationary period—I could approach him without fear of retaliation. By that time, what I held in my right hand amounted to no more than a scrawny scrub brush, while the other held a reward of grapes or raisins. The job was officially mine.

A month or so later, my employers couldn't believe their eyes. I left what remained of the broom at the door, entered the enclosure, walked over to the middle and sat down cross-legged on the floor. Gibby climbed down from his perch, waddled over to me holding his hands above his head—as gibbons do when walking—and plopped down beside me. I patted the inside of my thigh, inviting him to climb into my lap so that I could feed him some grapes. He played the role of Mark Antony to my Cleopatra.

It didn't take very long for me to realize that my animal coworkers had also become my buddies. My concern for their welfare was much more than a job responsibility. I was particularly keen to know what they felt when put through their paces, so I volunteered as a subject for dozens of experiments that required being stuck with hypodermic needles. I mean, what are friends for?

Gibbons

are not monkeys. They are lesser apes—smaller, tailless relatives of chimpanzees, gorillas and orangutans. Gibbons live in the tropical forests of Southeast Asia. Aerial acrobats of the jungle canopy, they are famous for their long, loud and penetrating calls. All 18 gibbon species are threatened with extinction, largely due to habitat loss.

Data gathered by the researchers were electronic impulses that emanated from the animals' muscles. Each time a gibbon swung an arm forward while swinging to the next branch, or a spider monkey grasped the trunk of a tree it was climbing, or a chimpanzee stood to walk upright, a series of muscle fibers would fire, and the muscle activity was recorded as an electromyograph (EMG) on an oscilloscope. A sharp spike on the video screen indicated a muscle was in use; a flat line showed that it was dormant and not required for that particular movement. If the gluteus maximus of a chimpanzee or a human is called into action as the foot hits the ground, and the bony prominences of ape and human femurs look anything like that of Lucy—our three million-year-old ancestor from Ethiopia—then perhaps she used the same butt muscles to stand upright and walk as well. The same logic would apply to arm and shoulder musculature and the ability to climb trees. The data we gathered in the lab helped inform paleontologists regarding the physical relationships between species, as well as the evolutionary path toward *Homo sapiens*.

The oscilloscope received the electronic impulses from tiny wireless transmitters worn on the primates' backs and fed by fine wire electrodes inserted into the target muscles. Each wire had two strands, glued together and only slightly larger than a human hair in diameter, their bare tips carefully placed in the muscles via a fine point hypodermic needle. Putting the electrodes in place while the animal was awake was impossible. Very light anesthesia made it painless. The animal awakened with no more than four electrodes fed into a matchbook-sized transmitter, and each had his or her own t-shirt or pair of pants (necessary to protect the wires) specially tailored for the occasion. The typical session lasted less than an hour, then each of my newfound primate friends sat patiently as I removed the apparatus. A leisurely romp around the room, a mutual grooming session and a few extra pieces of fruit signaled the end of their work day.

So what exactly did they feel? Without the light anesthesia, which was required for the animals, I had needles inserted into my arms, shoulders, hips, rear, thighs, calves and feet, as well as under my scapula and behind my collarbone. The only time I felt any discomfort at all was when they decided to see what my gluteus minimus was up to. Three gluteal muscles power the human backside: the maximus, medius and minimus. The largest, the maximus, is the outermost and gives our rear ends their attractive shape. The medius is smaller and lies beneath it. The minimus is the smallest of the three, barely a muscle at all, and is buried right up against the pelvis. To hook an electrode inside the gluteus minimus required a four-inch-long hypodermic needle. Sounds scary, but, surprisingly, it did not hurt even though the tip had to hit the bone and then be drawn back just a hair to be sure that the wire would hold.

My domain was the Lab Office Building, where all the primates were housed. The Department of Anatomical Sciences, home to my bosses' offices, was on the other side of the campus. I didn't spend much time there, except for lunch breaks. One day, Dr. Susman decided to give me a personal tour of the department. Midway through, we came upon a pair of double doors held shut by a huge, no-nonsense padlock. There was just enough space between the doors for me to see what was inside. To say the contents were eclectic would have been cliché. Standing up against the opposite wall was a line of spears, bows, arrows and what looked like blowguns. Masks, headdresses and necklaces not only hung from the walls, they were piled atop one another

MOLLY, A SOUTH AMERICAN SPIDER MONKEY, AND ME, STONY BROOK UNIVERSITY, NY, 1981
PHOTO COURTESY OF STEPHEN NASH

on tables where wide-mouth jars and bottles also sat. They were filled with formalin or alcohol and packed with the preserved internal organs and other body parts of unknown creatures. In between the piles, every available square inch of tabletop was taken up by animal skulls, handcrafts, other artifacts, tall stacks of books, maps and assorted documents.

"Wow, that's incredible! Whose stuff is this?"

"Oh, that's Mittermeier's crap."

MY DAUGHTER, MELANIE, FEEDING A BROWN LEMUR, STONY BROOK UNIVERSITY, NY, 1981

"Mittermeier?" Had I heard correctly? "As in Russ Mittermeier?"

"Yes, Russ. You know him?"

I'd read that he worked for the World Wildlife Fund, so I figured he was in Washington, DC. I would soon learn that he hung his hat at Stony Brook and that would change my life in a significant way. First, however, let me tell you a story about a very special chimpanzee.

LESSON LEARNED:
The plans we make and the career paths we choose should evolve as we evolve. If Charles Darwin taught us anything, it's that adapting to change is an enduring strength.

KENTON AND ME CLIMBING A TREE, STONY BROOK UNIVERSITY, NEW YORK, 1981
PHOTO COURTESY OF DR. RANDALL SUSMAN

JAILBREAK

Now we must redefine tool, redefine Man,
or accept chimpanzees as humans.

Telegram from Louis Leakey to Jane Goodall
regarding her discovery that the chimpanzees of Gombe
were observed to fashion and use simple tools
when "fishing" for termites (1960)

I reached for the branch just above me, glancing downward to confirm that Kenton was on my heels, keeping pace as we climbed higher in the oak tree. Had he decided to descend, to leave me and maybe mingle with the students milling on the mall, I'd probably have lost my job. But, our little adventure was well worth the risk. I'd been working with this amazing chimpanzee for a couple of years at that point, anticipating his moods and actions, and had a good sense of what he was likely to do next. I felt in control of the situation despite the fact that Kenton was in no way physically restrained. He wore no collar or harness and I held no leash. Physical restraint really would have been a joke anyway. Holding a leash on a chimpanzee in a tree? Who exactly is in control? Who's more likely to be found limp and dangling from a branch? Not the chimpanzee, my friend! No, as long as Kenton stayed close and quiet, as long as no one noticed us, our romp in the treetops was positive reinforcement for him. It was a reward for good behavior. Breaking him out of "jail" was the least I could do for my buddy.

For almost five years, I spent almost as much time with Kenton as I did with my wife and kids. That might be an exaggeration, but not by much.

KENTON, STONY BROOK UNIVERSITY, NEW YORK, 1981

Kenton was born at Georgia's Yerkes Primate Center, initially a subject in a sign language study. Researchers were making remarkable strides at the time, teaching apes to converse with humans by speaking with their hands. Unfortunately, Kenton "flunked out" of the program at an early age. While other young

chimpanzees might have been better candidates for those particular studies, Kenton's overall personality and demeanor toward human handlers were exemplary. His research career was quickly salvaged when he was sent north to Stony Brook, where he quickly became the most popular of all the resident nonhuman primates. By the time I came on board as the new primate technician, he was already well settled in.

Kenton and I stopped climbing at about 30 feet above the ground and scanned the terrain below. Only minutes before, I had unlocked the chain-link door to his enclosure so that he might join me in an adventure outside. Kenton and his companion, a younger captive-born male chimpanzee named Lester, shared two fairly spacious rooms. In their quarters they were able to run, climb, jump and take full advantage of the liberal space provided. Still, their world was man-made and ripe for any natural accoutrements I could provide.

I felt strongly that the primates under my care deserved to experience as much of the outside world as I was able to offer. The scientists to whom I directly reported were in full agreement and respected my judgment, so it was our little secret. Taking calculated risks like this tree-climbing adventure helped me develop confidence in my training strategy, as well as my ability to anticipate Kenton's behavior. There really was no choice except for the two of us to be "just a tad naughty" every now and then. At the very least, I felt that a chimpanzee should be able to climb trees as well as I could.

Kenton and I sat quietly for a few minutes, savoring the light summer breeze and soaking in rays of sunlight that filtered through the leaves. He took in his surroundings, watching everything and everyone in the distance. Eventually, it came time for us to sneak back into the lab, so we descended the oak tree undetected, hopped onto the loading dock and quickly scooted back down the hallway. When I unlocked the door to the chimpanzees' enclosure, Lester couldn't greet us quickly enough. (Though I would have loved to have taken Lester on these excursions, the fact of the matter was that I feared he might bolt.) The three of us sat on the floor together, grunting and enjoying a mutual grooming session. Both chimps eagerly picked through my beard, the hair on my arms and the top of my head, and I returned the favor. Occasionally, I'd pretend to find a flea, pop it in my mouth and smack my lips with feigned delight.

As a teenager, I'd read Dr. Jane Goodall's books, *My Friends the Wild Chimpanzees* and *In the Shadow of Man*, and watched the National Geographic television special about her groundbreaking research in Tanzania's then Gombe Stream Game Reserve. Of all the chimpanzees she described, my favorite was Mike, a rowdy son of a gun. Mike learned that by tossing empty kerosene cans around the field camp and hooting loudly, he could intimidate all the rival male chimps. For years, he'd been low chimp on the totem pole, but his loud and fearsome display quickly rocketed him upwards in the hierarchy. By acting out and creating a commotion, he made the quantum leap to the top.

One day in my high school library, after diving into one of Dr. Goodall's books, I felt inspired to "audition" for the role of Mike. A couple of empty cardboard boxes sat in the corner of the room, perfect props for kerosene cans. I took a deep breath and began to morph into a chimpanzee. Bending slightly at the waist, bowing my legs and hunching my shoulders

Visitors

to Disney's Animal Kingdom who stroll past the Tree of Life will encounter the image of David Greybeard, a very special chimp. David Greybeard was the first wild chimp at Tanzania's Gombe Stream National Park to accept Dr. Jane Goodall's presence in the forest and it was to him that she dedicated her first field research publications.

JANE GOODALL & MICHAEL EISNER AT THE DAVID GREYBEARD SCULPTURE, 1998
PHOTO COURTESY OF WALT DISNEY COMPANY

so that my arms hung closer to the floor, I swaggered over to the boxes, tilted my head down and swung my torso and arms with each small step. Reaching the "kerosene cans," I grunted quietly, picked up one in each hand and slowly turned around. Through pursed lips, guttural hooting sounds emerged from my throat, coupled with quickening bouts of deeply inhaled air. My hoots grew louder and more powerful. Had I been covered in hair, it would have been standing on end. I swung the boxes wildly from side to side and charged nothing in particular. Just before slamming into the opposite wall, I let the boxes fly and unleashed a scream.

Needless to say, my conduct was unacceptable by high school library standards. However, had the other students been chimpanzees, they would have rushed to me, panting and bowing in submission, and begging for reassurance that all was well. Even the librarian would have had to acknowledge my new rank. But we weren't chimpanzees and we were half a world away from an African forest. The librarian reached down, plucked the eyeglasses that hung from the chain around her neck and placed them on the bridge of her nose, I guess to get a good look at the ruckus-maker. Then she pursed her lips and shot her index finger straight up in front of her face—the universal sign for "Quiet, please!"

Decades later, I would never have thought of launching into such a performance. That type of aggressive and challenging behavior would have been totally inappropriate in my relationship with Kenton and Lester. Instead, positive reinforcement and composure were the rules and they turned out to be wonderful preparation for Kenton's eventual acting career. Word of Stony Brook's personable and talented ape gradually leaked to the media and brought the Children's Television Network to our door—Kenton's first offer for an acting role. The network asked if he might play himself in an episode of *3-2-1 Contact* that would require two full days of filming. Kenton costarred with a child actor who played Paco. Professor Susman played himself: a scientist who studies chimpanzees and other primates to learn more about human origins. The story line was simple: A young boy, Paco, meets a chimpanzee while taking a stroll along the beach (because sure, that just happens, right?) and is invited to spend some time with his new friend at the University. As I recall, Kenton accepted the role without any hesitation and never once asked, "What's my motivation?"

Kenton and Paco spent the entire morning romping around the gym together. This was new terrain for Kenton, but he had no problem mastering one apparatus after the other. He got to test the rings, the high bar, the balance beam and the pommel horse and seemed capable of competing with the most highly accomplished human athletes on each. Paco did his best to keep up but was clearly outmatched by his new simian friend.

At one point, the young boy and the chimpanzee hung by their arms, side-by-side on the high bar. The chimp was all arms, the boy all legs. The video camera rolled. All that the director wanted the two primates to do was to continue hanging for just a few seconds longer. Standing beside the cameraman, I nodded my approval to Kenton for remaining stationary and held up my hand, palm facing him, to indicate that he hold that position. He stared straight ahead, seeming to understand, but I noticed an impish—perhaps "chimpish"—look on his face. As the cameraman zoomed out from the scene, Kenton decided it was time for some improvisation. He reached over with his left foot and used his finger-length toes to grasp the cuff of the boy's blue jeans. A quick tug pulled Paco off the bar and onto the mats on the floor. He rolled over and laughed while Kenton remained hanging and stared straight into the camera. You could almost hear the clever ape say, "Well, I guess that's a wrap! Where's lunch?"

Word of Kenton's acting debut soon spread internationally. Famed scientist and broadcaster Dr. David Suzuki contacted the folks at Stony Brook to see if Kenton would be available for the final segment of *The Chain of Life*, his show on the Canadian Broadcasting Corporation. Dr. Suzuki and his crew flew in from British Columbia for the filming. We spent the morning and much of the afternoon in the lab until all but the final scene was "in the can" as they say.

Dr. Suzuki headed outside to finish up. He sat at a table, pen and paper in hand. As he tweaked his closing monologue, he looked up at me and asked, "Can you have Kenton simply sit down right here beside me for the last scene?" I nodded. A large rock and a line of tall trees formed the backdrop—the same trees Kenton and I often climbed together.

Dr. Suzuki rehearsed his remarks two or three times, then entered the scene and sat down beside Kenton. I signaled to Kenton to remain still. Dr. Suzuki looked into the camera and launched into his summary. Kenton sat quietly beside him, sometimes looking at his companion, sometimes gazing off into the surroundings and every so often looking into the camera. Dr. Suzuki emphasized the importance of both field and laboratory research that explores the similarities between humans and apes. He pointed out that new discoveries about our evolutionary relationships continue to be made.

As if on cue, Kenton's eyes focused on the camera straight ahead.

Dr. Suzuki added, "And based on the results of these research efforts …"

Kenton slowly swung his hairy arm around Dr. Suzuki's neck, his hand coming to rest on his new friend's shoulder. My eyebrows inched upward.

"… we very well may find …"

With a gentle tug, Kenton drew his companion closer and leaned into him. The chimpanzee's head rested gently against that of the scientist, their faces cheek to cheek. Both were looking directly into the lens. I bit my lip.

"… that our wild cousins are actually *much* more closely related to us …"

And that's when Dr. Suzuki lost it. Kenton's impeccable improv was just too much for the good doctor who started laughing and could barely say the words in the last line.

"… than we ever could have imagined."

My head dropped and I thought to myself, "Kenton nailed it. We were so close!"

The cameraman asked politely, "Can we try that again? I need a clean take."

"We'll give it a shot," was all I could muster in response. Unfortunately, Kenton and I had no hand signals for "Okay, buddy, now hug the host tighter" or "Try scrunching up together just a tad closer." My only hope was that, if he'd done it once, he might just do it again. But I was wrong. Despite several retakes, I just couldn't persuade Kenton to repeat his earlier performance on cue.

The real shame is that the original footage somehow disappeared and has never been found. It would have made the perfect blooper.

The best part about my work with Kenton was being able to share his charm with others. One weekend, when my daughter Melanie was four years old, I brought her to the University to meet the chimps. Kenton was eight or nine at the time and weighed close to 100 pounds. Lester was about two-thirds his size. I was well aware of a chimpanzee's incredible strength and of the potential for unanticipated changes in an ape's behavior. At the same time, I knew my chimps pretty well. Positive interactions with friends and strangers alike were powerful rewards that reinforced continuing good behavior. Having said that, these encounters always demanded my complete and unbroken attention to ensure the safety of everyone involved.

Melanie sat on the floor in a room that I often used for play sessions with the chimps. I brought in Kenton and Lester and let them greet her. Both did so with a hug. Despite being dwarfed and outnumbered by her new friends, my little girl was unafraid. She patted and hugged them back. Had she shown any fear or had either chimp displayed even the slightest sign of aggression, I would have ended the introduction immediately.

KENTON AND MELANIE, STONY BROOK UNIVERSITY, NEW YORK, 1981

Kenton and Lester set the agenda. Having politely greeted their new playmate, they began to conduct a thorough physical inspection of my daughter: her hair, face, ears, hands, arms and legs, her sweatshirt, pants and shoes. It seemed important that they touch every part of her, as well as each piece of clothing, and then bring their fingers to their noses afterward each time for a sniff. Melanie tolerated this well enough but apparently didn't feel any need to reciprocate. Eventually, she tired of the inspection, stood up and walked away. Just as quickly, Kenton rose from his haunches and placed his hands on Melanie's hips. Lester then joined them, latching onto Kenton's backside. In unison, the three of them began a slow march across the room—a most unusual Conga line. The only things missing were someone beating a drum or shaking maracas and Carmen Miranda bringing up the rear with a fruit-filled hat on her head.

A number of people, including family and friends, have asked me whether I took too much of a chance with Melanie's safety that day. It's a legitimate question. The answer is always no, but I probably would never do something like that again. Nan accepts my answer, understanding that I would never do anything that I felt might put our children at risk. Our trust in one another's judgment comes from having survived an ordeal years before that was well beyond our control.

It's what sent us on that road trip across the country with no predetermined destination. Nan and I lost our first child, Scott, when he was only 15 months old. He is the brother that Melanie and Evan know today only through photos. Scotty was born with a terminal genetic disease. He never walked, talked, learned to crawl or turned over in his crib. The disease left him lacking a critical enzyme, one that breaks down a fat that helps the body maintain a healthy nervous system. Minus that enzyme, the fat rises to toxic levels. It accumulates in different tissues and organs and ultimately destroys them. In the most severe cases, infants suffer from enlarged livers and spleens and are prone to seizures.

A stricken child appears to develop normally up until about six months of age, but then his or her condition noticeably deteriorates. Blindness and deafness inevitably set in before the age of two, which many do not reach. Baby teeth may never break through their gums. Then comes the day when food can no longer be taken by mouth, only through a stomach tube that's inserted down the nose. Several times a day, parents heavily pat their baby's back and chest with cupped hands to clear a path to the lungs, which become increasingly congested as the disease progresses. The harsh reality is that each new day is just a little bit worse than the day before and then suddenly the body's organs just completely collapse; such was our Scotty's fate. He passed in 1978. A cure for the disease, one of several conditions known as lipid storage disorders, is still elusive. According to medical

SCOTT KONSTANT, MASTIC BEACH, NEW YORK, 1977

authorities, one in every 5,000 to 10,000 children born around the world each year will suffer from a disease of this nature.

I first met Kenton three years after Nan and I lost Scotty. The years Kenton and I worked together were filled with discovery and friendship. Saying goodbye wasn't easy. In 1986, I left my job on Long Island and moved with my family to Philadelphia.

Kenton, Lester and my other primate buddies remained with the research program, but a couple of years later I learned that Kenton had retired from his research duties to a small private zoo in the Carolinas. We never reunited, but I will always be grateful for his friendship and the fact that he accepted me as a surrogate chimpanzee.

Since my animal training days and my adventures with Kenton, my career in primate conservation has blossomed, especially when it comes to providing support for efforts that benefit wild chimpanzees. Some of my projects have included field research, monitoring and protection, tropical forest management, the creation of national parks and other conservation areas, the development of national and regional conservation action plans, and support for sanctuaries that sustain orphaned chimpanzees rescued from trafficking. In some cases—not very many, unfortunately—these animals can be rehabilitated and returned to the wild. I'm very proud to say that, in total, I have had the opportunity to direct more than one million dollars in support of chimpanzee conservation projects in more than 20 African countries.

LESSON LEARNED:
Shared DNA of 95% or more with an ape can help create strong bonds of friendship and compassion between our species, paling in comparison only to the much stronger bonds that exist between a parent and a child.

RUSSELL MITTERMEIER TRACKING MONKEYS IN THE PERUVIAN ANDES, 1983
PHOTO COURTESY OF ANDREW L. YOUNG

RUSSELL
OF THE
APES

*His life among these fierce apes had been happy; for his
recollections held no other life, nor did he know that there existed
within the universe aught else than his little forest and
the wild jungle animals with which he was familiar.*

Edgar Rice Burroughs, *Tarzan of the Apes* (1914)

Okay, so where did I leave off regarding my hopes of one day meeting the iconic Dr. Russell Mittermeier?

I'd been working with primates at Stony Brook for a month or so and my boss, Dr. Susman, was taking me on a tour of the anatomy department. He had just informed me that a large storehouse full of jungle artifacts, biological specimens, and the like belonged to Russ Mittermeier, who I had no idea had anything to do with the University.

"This is Russ Mittermeier's room? I've never met him, but I sure would like to. I mean, if we're both talking about the same Russ Mittermeier." I took another peek between the two doors. "What's all this stuff doing here? A while back, I read that he works for the World Wildlife Fund, so I figured he lived in DC."

Dr. Susman explained, "He does work for WWF, but he's also an adjunct professor here at Stony Brook and actually lives close by. The University gives him office space." As he gestured toward the room, he added, "Russ is like a ghost. He comes in at night and stuff just keeps piling up in there."

That partially explained why our paths had yet to cross. I tried not to appear too eager, "Can you introduce me to him? I'd like to learn more about his work."

"Sure, you'll definitely get to meet him. You're just going to have to wait. I think he's down in Brazil right now and due back in a couple of months."

Someone else in the department had Russ's travel schedule and shared his return date with me. Fast forward two months.

Now that I knew Dr. Mittermeier's routine, I left work at my normal quitting time and made the 20-mile drive back home for dinner with Nan, Melanie and Evan, the newest addition to the family. After we ate and visited, Nan sent me back to Stony Brook, planting a kiss on my cheek for good luck. I parked my car in the lot that had largely emptied out a couple of hours before, took the elevator up to the fifth floor, walked down the hall and waited outside the double doors of Russ's storeroom. Occasionally, I glanced toward the elevator.

At a few minutes past eight o'clock, a shaggy-haired man with a tropical tan, wearing a short-sleeved safari shirt emerged from the elevator. He was hefting a large, overloaded leather handbag in one hand and an extra-large Styrofoam cup of coffee in the other. As he approached the stranger standing outside his door, he looked up with the healthy dose of suspicion you'd expect from someone born and raised in the South Bronx.

"Dr. Mittermeier?" I reached out reflexively to shake his hand, not thinking about how he was supposed to respond with both hands already occupied. "I'm Bill Konstant. I'm new in the department. They told me the best way to meet you was to come here at night, and you'd eventually show up."

"Well, whoever told you that knows me pretty well." Russ smiled, gently placing the coffee cup on the floor so that we could shake hands. "When I'm in the field, I work during the day just like everyone else, but when I'm back here in the States, I'm strictly nocturnal."

He unlocked the door and I followed him inside, watching as he laid the bag on the floor in what appeared to be the only space available. "I've just spent the last couple of months in Brazil's Atlantic forest setting up some field surveys and working on some other projects." He pointed to the leather bag. "These are just some of the goodies I've brought back." Russ quickly walked out of the room, motioning for me to follow. "Come on, we can talk in my office." Man, that was great to hear: the man had an office. There was no way anyone could have worked where we were standing.

A few yards down the hall, he unlocked a second door, this one to a much smaller room. Like the first, this room was also nearly filled to the brim, but in this case, with books, periodicals, envelopes and stacks of paper. An IBM Selectric typewriter sat in the middle of his desk with just enough space beside it to accommodate an extra-large cup of coffee. The typewriter itself sported dried coffee blotches. He only had one chair and it was occupied by a stack of books, so we both remained standing.

Russ led. "So, why are you so eager to meet me?"

Had I thought to bring the World Wildlife Fund newsletter, I would only have had to hold it up for him to guess the reason. I'm not sure how many times others had expressed their desire to work with him, but I'm guessing it was more than just a few. On the spot, I offered to volunteer my time. Since I was there at the University during the day, I could give him my lunch break or maybe stay an extra hour after work. His face conveyed both appreciation and skepticism. For all he knew, I was just a groupie or some kook.

"If you can stay late for a half-hour or so tomorrow afternoon, I'll pull together a list of projects that might be of interest. Can you write?"

"Yeah, I can write." I received a decent score on the verbal section of my SATs if that meant anything. Otherwise, I really had no meaningful experience.

"Okay! I'll see you tomorrow at about five o'clock." We shook hands again and I drove home to tell Nan that there was a chance she and the kids might be seeing a bit less of me in the months ahead.

Russ and I met in his office the next day as planned. As I walked in, he grabbed a book from his desk. "*International Zoo Yearbook*, ever seen it?" I nodded. "I've been asked to prepare an article about returning primates from captivity to the wild. Maybe you could help me write it? The deadline's a few months away, so there's no rush, but some research needs to be done first and that will take some time."

The paper that

Russ and I coauthored included the story of spider monkeys reintroduced to Barro Colorado Island following construction of the Panama Canal. In the early 1900s, the damning of the Chagres River created Gatun Lake and turned Barro Colorado, a forested mountain within this primate's range, into an island. In the 1950s and 1960s, the Smithsonian Institution's Tropical Research Institute acquired spider monkeys from Panama City markets and released them into these hill forests.

It hadn't been 24 hours since we met, and Russ was asking me to coauthor a scientific paper. I was blown away. "That would be great!"

PANAMANIAN SPIDER MONKEY, SUMMIT ZOO, PANAMA, 2007

"Good! Then there's something else I'm going to need help with. Let me show you." We took a walk back to his storage room. On the table was a large glass jar packed with the innards of some creatures that had met their end in a South American rain forest.

PRIMATOLOGIST RUSS MITTERMEIER AND A YOUNG ORANGUTAN, 1979
PHOTO COURTESY OF RUSSELL MITTERMEIER

"These stomachs are from bearded saki monkeys shot by hunters in Suriname." Russ had retrieved about a half-dozen stomachs from the hunters (who had no interest in them), tied off the ends of each and preserved the organs in alcohol for further study. "I did my doctoral dissertation research in Suriname, studying how different primate species divide the available resources. It's a field of study called synecology. Bearded sakis eat seeds and nuts. Their jaws are incredibly powerful and can crack the hardest shells, like Brazil nuts. I think they probably also eat insects, but no one has ever documented that. How would you like to help me prove that they do?"

The task was right up my alley. I'd done dozens of dissections in college and a number of necropsies—animal autopsies—during my zoo days. "Sure! I can get started on it right away." It wasn't the ideal lunchtime project, but what the hell.

I was still holding down a full-time job in Stony Brook's Department of Anatomical Sciences and taking courses toward my master's degree when Russ officially brought me on board as his part-time assistant at the World Wildlife Fund in early 1983. In April of that year, Bob Suter, one of Russ's high school buddies, wrote a feature article, "Russell of the Apes," for Newsday's *Sunday Magazine*. It began, "When he was a teenager hunting turtles, snakes and lizards in Long Island's swamps and creeks, Russell Mittermeier learned the importance of conservation. He later became one of the world's leading experts on primate conservation, and now devotes his life to saving apes, monkeys and lemurs from extinction." The article featured a two-page spread, at the center of which was that iconic photo of a shaggy human holding a shaggy young orangutan that had been rescued from the illegal pet trade. It also made known that, from the time he was a young boy, Russ imagined himself as Tarzan of the Jungle, much the same as I envisioned myself as Mowgli from *The Jungle Book*.

The orphaned

young orangutan pictured with Russ came to the Sepilok Orangutan Rehabilitation Center in Sabah, Malaysia in the late 1970s, rescued from a logging site, plantation or life as an illegal family pet. The Rehabilitation Center was established in 1964 in a rain forest reserve near the city of Sandakan. Over the decades, several dozen rehabilitated orangutans have moved from the sanctuary to the surrounding forests which are now protected.

Nan and I sometimes joke that Russ almost destroyed our marriage. A couple of months before "Russell of the Apes" hit the newsstands, he asked me to accompany him on a month-long trip to Brazil. It took a fair amount of persuading to convince Nan that this wouldn't totally disrupt our lives. I had arranged for time off from my primate technician job and taken care of my academic responsibilities in advance, so that wasn't an issue. However, while I was playing Indiana Jones, wielding a machete and bushwhacking my way through vine tangles in South American jungles, she would be holding down her own job as a registered nurse and caring for two small children, ages four and one, all by herself for a month.

My decision to seize this opportunity of a lifetime could easily have been the first complaint in any divorce papers that Nan might have decided to serve me, and I admit that there would have been little to offer in defense. Instead, she gave me her blessing to embark upon my first rain forest adventure. In return, I promised to write her a letter every day that I was away. Reading through those letters together nearly 40 years later brought back wonderful memories for both of us.

LESSON LEARNED:
Pushing the envelope, burning the candle at both ends and working outside one's comfort zone—if these don't kill you— are excellent ways to test your resolve and shape your career, especially if you can stomach, so to speak, some monkey innards along the way.

YOUNG ORANGUTAN, SEPILOK SANCTUARY, SANDAKAN, MALAYSIA, 2006

MURIQUI, FAZENDA MONTES CLAROS, MINAS GERAIS, BRAZIL, 1999

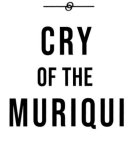

CRY
OF THE
MURIQUI

Everyone admires
The monkey who walks on its feet
The monkey was once human
It can walk as it desires!

Luis da Camara Cascudo, *Superstitions of Brazil* (1985)
as quoted in *Faces in the Forest* by Karen Strier (1992)

A large, male, chocolate-brown howler monkey led his family troop of six through the forest. The date was May 7, 1983, and these were the first monkeys I had ever laid eyes on in the wild. We were hiking the last remaining forests around a coffee plantation and cattle ranch just outside the small town of Caratinga in the Brazilian state of Minas Gerais. Fazenda Montes Claros—the Farm in the Clear Mountains—was owned by Feliciano Miguel Abdalla, the son of a Lebanese immigrant. Senhor Feliciano had taken it upon himself to protect hundreds of acres of pristine tropical forest, while many of his neighbors had felled their small forest patches for the valuable timber. Feliciano was proud that his property was home to the largest population of muriqui monkeys known at the time—an estimated 100 individuals.

The muriqui (pronounced moor-ee-KEE), previously called the woolly spider monkey, is the largest of all South American primates. It lives only within a thin strip of coastal forest: the

111

BROWN HOWLER MONKEYS, FAZENDA MONTES CLAROS, 2021
PHOTO COURTESY OF CARLA POSSAMAI

Atlantic Forest region of Brazil. The muriquis of Montes Claros share their forests with three other monkeys: brown howlers, tufted capuchins and buffy-headed marmosets. I checked off all three before I finally caught a fleeting glimpse of a muriqui's *bunda*—backend—moving up and away through the forest canopy and disappearing into a backdrop of branches and leaves.

Muriquis are not only the largest Brazilian primates but are among the most endangered. A mature male can tip the scales at 30 pounds, making it a valued source of protein and a favored target of hunters for centuries. This monkey's long toes are excellent for grasping, while shortened thumbs allow its hands to serve as hooks for swinging or hanging below branches. A prehensile tail acts like a fifth limb for suspension. The muriqui's ability to move swiftly and deftly through high levels of the forest offers it some advantage in avoiding hunters, but little

TUFTED CAPUCHIN MONKEY, FAZENDA MONTES CLAROS, 2021
PHOTO COURTESY OF CARLA POSSAMAI

BUFFY-HEADED MARMOSET, FAZENDA MONTES CLAROS, 2022
PHOTO COURTESY OF CARLA POSSAMAI

THE MURIQUI IS THE LARGEST SOUTH AMERICAN MONKEY, FAZENDA MONTES CLAROS, MINAS GERAIS, BRAZIL, 1999

defense against a growing army of human settlers. More than 90 percent of Brazil's Atlantic forests have disappeared since the arrival of Portuguese colonists in the early 1500s. Valuable Brazilian hardwoods (South American walnut, cherry, oak, teak and tigerwood trees) were cut to make fine furniture, while trees of lesser value were felled for general construction and charcoal production, or just cleared and burned where they lay to accommodate an expanding agricultural frontier. Whatever the muriquis' population was prior to the arrival of Europeans, biologists believe that their numbers have declined as steeply as their home forests, by 90 percent or more.

When I first traveled to Brazil in 1983, primatologists believed that only one species of muriqui existed. Today, biologists recognize two distinct types: a northern, freckle-faced and a southern, charcoal-faced. The states of São Paulo and Paraná are home to the southern muriqui; northern muriqui populations extend northeast into the state of Bahia. Both species live in the states of Rio de Janeiro, Espírito Santo and Minas Gerais (the latter is where I had my first sighting).

You're more likely to hear this monkey before you see it. Its unique horse-like whinny gives it away even at a distance. This is the cry of the muriquis. But zeroing in on the animals themselves can still be difficult. In the early 1980s, the muriquis of Fazenda Montes Claros were becoming familiar with a human presence beyond that of Senhor Feliciano, his family and their farm workers. Professors and students from Brazilian and US universities began launching field studies which led to the creation of a bona fide research station on-site.

My visit to Montes Claros coincided with a very special event: the dedication of the Feliciano Miguel Abdalla Ecological Station, a base camp for scientists nestled next to the surrounding forests. Close to 100 people flocked to the Station for the Feast of the Muriqui. Large slabs of beef were skewered on bamboo spears, roasted over open-pit fires, and washed down with glasses of beer, sugarcane alcohol and Kool-Aid. An old man pumped away on his accordion and kept everyone's feet tapping, while crews from Brazil's major television networks set up for interviews. After the sun disappeared beyond the forested hillside, we all watched *Cry of the Muriqui*, a 25-minute film produced for the World Wildlife Fund. Russ had recruited Andy Young, a Harvard undergraduate student from Chappaqua, New York to produce the film, grab the public's attention and raise funds for this incredible monkey's preservation.

Later that year, Dr. Karen Strier of the University of Wisconsin-Madison took up residence at the ecological station. She launched a tropical forest research program and a primate conservation initiative, both of which continue to this day.

PRIMATE FIELD RESEARCH STATION, FAZENDA MONTES CLAROS, 1983

Her book about the adventure, *Faces in the Forest*, delves into her and her Brazilian team's groundbreaking studies—research that led to the creation of the 2,500-acre Feliciano Miguel Abdalla Private Natural Heritage Reserve. After Senhor Feliciano passed away in 2000, his family created a nonprofit organization, Preserve-Muriqui, to manage this newly protected area. Today, primate enthusiasts from around the world travel to the sleepy mountain town of Caratinga for the chance to view the several hundred muriquis that call the forests of Montes Claros home.

During our month in Brazil, Russ and I visited the Rio de Janeiro Primate Center, where I met Coimbra, the late Dr. Adelmar Coimbra-Filho, Father of Brazilian Primatology. The Center, tucked away in the hill forests of the Serra dos Órgãos Mountains, is home to at least two dozen Brazilian primate species. Most prominent among them are golden, black and golden-headed lion tamarins—squirrel-sized monkeys unfortunately highly prized for the illegal pet trade. Also on-site at the time, in a makeshift enclosure, were a couple of muriquis that authorities had confiscated. Since they couldn't be released into the wild, this was the next best place for them. Researchers hoped their offspring could repopulate protected forests.

Several months before we left the States, Russ put me in touch with Coimbra and his assistant, Claudio Padua, and asked them to develop plans for a special muriqui facility. They had construction drawings prepared and the ground was already broken, but the project was not yet fully funded. That was my job, raising the balance needed. First stop: a zoo conference in Vancouver, British Columbia. My presentation's title was "Captive Breeding of the Muriqui in Brazil: A Role for American Zoos."

Very little was

known about the muriqui when I traveled to Brazil in 1983. The species was believed to number in the low hundreds and was protected within only five biological reserves, state parks and privately-owned forests. Four decades of field research have discovered many new populations and bumped estimated numbers to more than 2,000 animals living throughout 35 forests, of which at least a dozen are protected.

SENHOR FELICIANO MIGUEL ABDALLA (LEFT) DEDICATES THE PRIMATE FIELD RESEARCH STATION, FAZENDA MONTES CLAROS, 1983

The Vancouver conference was a really big deal—my first time in front of a large audience without a sea lion backup, as well as my first time asking for money. No one passed the hat after a sea lion show. The serious challenge of fundraising made me nervous. I anticipated much greater scrutiny from the audience, so I began practicing my talk weeks before the conference. I also felt myself developing an acute case of *glossophobia,* the fear of public speaking. Apparently, this is the most common fear of all, greater than the fear of heights, spiders or even death. Glossophobia affects nearly three out of every four people. I've since learned that folks like Abraham Lincoln, Thomas Jefferson, Winston Churchill and even Harrison Ford share this same trepidation. Yet somehow it didn't matter that I was in such good company.

RUSS AND ME, LUNCH AND LAUGHS ON A BRAZILIAN RAIN FOREST TRAIL, 1983
PHOTO COURTESY OF ISABEL CONSTABLE

My presentation was scheduled for the first day of the conference, which I considered a blessing. Get my talk out of the way as soon as possible. There were five speakers in all, the other four were career professionals from the Bronx, National and San Diego Zoos. I was a newbie. We took the stage in the first afternoon session, which gave me the chance to listen to a few talks that morning and gauge the general caliber of presentations. No one knocked my socks off. Still, I was a Nervous Nellie and needed reassurance, so I decided to chat up a couple of friends to see if they might offer some remedy for my jitters. So, here's how it went:

Good afternoon, folks.

I'm going to speak to you today about efforts to save the largest and one of the most endangered monkeys in all of South America, a monkey called the muriqui. First, however, I need to confess and apologize for my fear of being up here on stage in front of you. This morning, I was scared to death, feeling like I just might lose it. So I decided to ask two close friends, both good speakers, what they do to calm their nerves before giving a talk. The first friend told me that he goes for a run, maybe for half an hour. It relieves tension. The other one told me that he has a drink, just one beer or a glass of wine, and that works well for him. Both strategies sounded reasonable. But I just couldn't decide which would work best for me. As a result, I spent the last half-hour downtown running from one bar to the next.

Okay, it didn't bring down the house, but it did get a few laughs and certainly broke the ice for me. It also taught me a good lesson. My sense of humor, warped as it may be at times, was a reliable tool in a pinch.

I spent the next 14 minutes sharing images from my trip. It helped that so few people in the audience—perhaps none—had ever seen a live muriqui. I'm also guessing that most hadn't been to Brazil. Several friends came up afterward to congratulate me as I gathered up my papers and slides. I thanked them for their kind words and was just about to head back to my hotel room when a bespectacled gentleman with a neatly-trimmed reddish beard intercepted me in the lobby. His name was Jon Jensen, then executive director of Wildlife Preservation Trust International, a small organization based in Philadelphia, right across the street from the Zoo. Jon was very interested in the muriqui project. He gave me his card and asked that I send him a detailed proposal.

Several months later, the Trust awarded a $15,000 grant to Dr. Coimbra-Filho. Construction of the new muriqui facility at the Rio Primate Center was now paid for in full and I could carve the first notch in my fundraising belt. How this would impact my career in conservation wasn't immediately apparent, but it did provide an inkling of what might lie ahead.

LESSON LEARNED:
When you can't think of exactly what you'd like to say, injecting a good joke or a funny story might just be the ticket. For me, it can't hurt.

LITTLE LIONS
OF
BRAZIL

*"Everybody's Got Something to Hide
Except for Me and My Monkey"*

The Beatles, *White Album* (1968)

I. GOLDEN-HEADED LION TAMARIN

The tiny monkey reminded me of Chips, my childhood pet squirrel, as it scampered down the arm of the tall Brazilian woman. It stopped at Cristina Alves' wrist beside the sunglasses she was holding, posing long enough for Russ and me to snap a few photos. Cristina was a biology student at Brazil's Federal University of Minas Gerais and the little primate on her arm was a young golden-headed lion tamarin. In the early 1980s, three lion tamarin species were known to science: the golden lion tamarin, golden-headed lion tamarin and black lion tamarin. A fourth, the black-faced lion tamarin, would stay hidden from scientists for nearly a decade longer. All are considered Endangered at some level on the IUCN List of Threatened Species—the world's bible, if you will, of threatened plants and animals. Lion tamarins are not found anywhere else in the world outside of Brazil's Atlantic Forest.

Cristina was one of several university students that I met during my first trip to Brazil. She was pursuing a career in primate conservation; her efforts focused on the golden-headed lion

CRISTINA ALVES AND A YOUNG GOLDEN-HEADED LION TAMARIN,
MINAS GERAIS, BRAZIL, 1983

tamarin in the coastal state of Bahia. Its tropical forest home
had been decimated and fragmented to the same degree
as had the muriqui's habitat. Unfortunately, the tamarin's

124

incredible cuteness has made it a prime target for the illegal pet trade for decades. The young rescued tamarin in front of me posed cooperatively for us on Cristina's arm and seemed quite content. You could easily see why the locals relished them as pets. As a victim of this practice, this tiny tamarin was now destined for a sanctuary.

In December 1984, Cristina visited Nan and me at our home in Bellport, New York. On the first morning of her stay, as the three of us savored our cups of coffee, the day was shaping up to be typical for early December on Long Island: some frost on the lawn and leaves, the temperature hovering at around freezing, but promising to reach into the high 40s or low 50s by noon.

Cristina politely excused herself from the table, rose from her seat and tiptoed over to the refrigerator. She slowly opened the freezer compartment and stared inside as wisps of icy air escaped, floating past her face. Then she tentatively reached inside and held her hand there.

Our guest had just returned from the English Channel island of Jersey where she had spent the late summer and early fall studying at the International Training Center for the Conservation and Captive Breeding of Endangered Species. Part of its mission is to reintroduce these animals into areas where their forest homes can be protected. Her focus was on South American monkeys, many of which had been born at the host institution, Gerald Durrell's world-famous Jersey Wildlife Preservation Trust. During her stay, however, Cristina also received training in the care and breeding of lemurs, orangutans and a variety of reptiles. And she had the honor of meeting Princess Anne, a Royal Patron of the Trust, to whom she made a brief presentation regarding her lion tamarin project back home in Brazil.

With the Long Island late autumn day unfolding, Cristina was still standing in front of my freezer. "Bill, does the temperature really drop below freezing in the winter here in New York *and* in England?"

"Well, if our freezer is working properly, what you're feeling should be close to zero degrees Fahrenheit, well below freezing. And yes, it does sometimes get that cold here and also where you were staying in England—not often, but sometimes. And then, if it's windy, the wind chill factor will bring the temperature down to what we like to call 'really friggin' cold.'"

Cristina withdrew her hand from the freezer and quickly shut the door. "If I had stayed there, I would have frozen to death! I can't wait to go home."

The next year, Cristina invited Nan and me to visit her in Brazil. She was already hard at work in Bahia, creating Fundação Pau Brasil (the Brazilwood Foundation), a small non-profit organization named after the national tree. The Foundation's first initiative, Projeto Mico-Leão Baiano (the Bahian Lion Tamarin Project), focused on saving this endangered species.

Germany's

Alexander Philip Maximilian, the Prince of Wied-Neuwied, made the first field observations of lion tamarins in the early 1800s during his travels through Brazil's Atlantic coastal forests. At the time, he described golden-headed lion tamarins as common. Today, scientists believe that perhaps no more than 6,000 individuals exist, only a third of their estimated numbers at the turn of the century. The golden-headed lion tamarin is listed as Endangered.

Like the other lion tamarins, the golden-headed species survives on a diet of ripe fruits, flowers, nectar, plant exudates (gums) and a

GOLDEN-HEADED LION TAMARIN, BAHIA, BRAZIL, 1990

variety of small animal prey: frogs, snails, lizards, spiders and insects. These inquisitive little monkeys use their long dexterous fingers to fish much of their prey from the water-filled leaves of bromeliads that carpet tropical tree limbs and branches. Lion tamarins live in small family groups, usually the two parents and their most recent offspring, which typically arrive as twins. Frequently, family groups will also include young from a previous litter but, in any given season, only one adult female will breed. Each evening, the entire family group retires to a sleeping nest. It might be a cavity in a tree trunk or a hollowed-out chamber in a mass of bromeliad roots.

The Una Biological Reserve is one of the last strongholds for the golden-headed lion tamarin. About one thousand—a small but significant percentage of the entire population—roam Una's nearly 50,000 acres. Tragically, in the 1980s, Bahia was losing forests equivalent in area to eight such reserves every single year. I saw the results of such a devastating loss firsthand, right on Una's perimeter. A blackened landscape was all that remained after the valuable timber had been cut and hauled away, and what still stood had been burned to the ground. Nature had not been entirely defeated though, as scattered seedlings—specks of green—had just begun to emerge from the charred ground. It was anemic evidence of what once was a lush forest. The chances of it ever being restored are likely nil.

Cristina's research determined that in areas where forest has partially yielded to agriculture, golden-headed lion tamarins appeared capable of eking out an existence on farms where crops like cacao are grown in the shade of a forest canopy. Cacao is the fruit from which cocoa is derived; it's a staple of Bahia's economy. Most farmers, however, clear-cut the original forest and sell the timber. The cash helps pay for the cacao seedlings and provides an income for a few years until the first harvest. They shade the seedlings by planting bananas or fast-growing exotic tree species. What remains is a ghost of the original forest.

The task for Cristina and her team of young volunteers was to bring word of an alternative production method to the region's more forward-thinking cacao farmers. The new method, called *cabruca*, does not involve clear-cutting. Instead, a significant

DEFORESTATION NEAR BAHIA'S UNA BIOLOGICAL RESERVE, 1990

number of the original trees are left standing to shade the cacao seedlings. By doing so, the farmers can maintain forest corridors through their properties—corridors that allow tamarins and other animals to travel from one forest patch to another. Under the cabruca system, cacao production typically increases, numerous bird and arboreal mammal species can find food in the treetops, and many farmers can register their properties as permanent private reserves for wildlife, providing tax incentives.

I had the opportunity to work closely with Cristina for several years, helping her raise support for a public awareness campaign and to rescue and care for pet tamarins. Brazil's national commission for cocoa production not only helped support these efforts but also introduced Cristina to Mars, Incorporated (the international company known for chocolate bars), which energized Cristina tremendously and helped take her programs to the next level.

The golden-headed lion tamarin's survival still hangs in the balance. However, it is the most abundant of all the lion tamarins, and its future is brighter due to the commitment of a growing team of Brazilian biologists following in Cristina's footsteps.

II. BLACK LION TAMARIN

Only twice in my life has someone suggested that I wear pantyhose. Neither time did I take offense, nor punch anyone in the nose. The first invitation came from Claudio Padua, assistant director of the Rio de Janeiro Primate Center, during my first travels to Brazil. Six years later, in 1989, we met again, not in Rio, but at the foot of Morro do Diabo (the Hill of the Devil) in the state of São Paulo. Claudio and I were preparing to enter the lowland forest surrounding the mountain. Ticks and chiggers infest the area, so Claudio pointed out that pantyhose were quite effective at keeping these obnoxious pests out of your drawers and away from your

privates. I politely declined his invitation, deciding instead just to tuck my pant legs into my socks and take my chances. The second time that someone suggested I wear pantyhose had nothing at all to do with ticks and chiggers, but that's a story for another time.

BLACK LION TAMARIN EDUCATIONAL POSTER
ARTWORK COURTESY OF STEPHEN NASH

Morro do Diabo State Park is one of the final strongholds for the black (or golden-rumped) lion tamarin. At slightly more than 800 animals, the Park's tamarins are the largest remaining sub-population of this species, which probably numbers about a thousand individuals. Incredibly, for much of the 20th century, the species was believed to be extinct. That was until 1970 when none other than Dr. Coimbra-Filho (Claudio's boss at the Primate Center) rediscovered the black lion tamarin at Morro do Diabo. Ensuring this tiny monkey's survival became a quest for Claudio, a biologist, and his wife, Suzana, who holds advanced degrees in education and sustainability. Their decision to pull up stakes in Rio and head south converted them into instant champions for this threatened monkey; they cofounded Projeto Mico-Leão Preto—The Black Lion Tamarin Project. You could say that their mission was not to let this precious primate "go extinct a second time."

After a short walk from the forest edge to the base of Morro do Diabo, Claudio sat on a rock ledge scanning the horizon, arms draped over a folded knee and hands clasped together. From the foot of the mountain, he looked out over the lowland tropical forest, a precious and dwindling landscape along Brazil's heavily populated Atlantic Coast. Legend has it that Morro do Diabo got its name centuries ago when indigenous tribes turned on early Portuguese pioneers and fortune hunters—the *bandeirantes*—dispatching them and leaving their bodies to rot. In the ensuing centuries, the entire region endured an ecological assault that continues to this day. The forests teemed with hunters and loggers who set up sawmills to process illegally harvested timber. Swarms of squatters and claim-jumpers followed. Pasture and cattle replaced trees. Forests gave way to savannas. By some miracle, a substantial chunk of forest surrounding the flat-topped mountain managed to survive. Its reputation as the Hill of the Devil ironically became a blessing.

SENHOR JOSE AND CLAUDIO, MORRO DO DIABO STATE PARK, 1989

Claudio and his assistant, Senhor José, led me through spindly cacti that climbed twisted tree trunks, their branches chock-full of with bromeliads and orchids. Deep within the tangled root masses of these plants, family groups of tiny black monkeys found sanctuary during the night, religiously entering and exiting their makeshift shelters in the same order each time. Each family group, a breeding pair and their dependent offspring, made use of several such shelters scattered throughout their range. Should the researchers need to, Claudio and Senhor José could cover the hole after the tamarins had entered for the night, and then capture an animal from each group the following morning to fit it with a tiny radio collar. The lightweight transmitter does not encumber the wearer, and the repetitive signal emitted by the device allows the field research team to track the daily movements of the whole family. Using this technique, Claudio and his team built a solid base of ecological and behavioral data for Morro do Diabo's tamarins. They then expanded the program to include previously unknown populations in the region.

Projeto Mico-Leão Preto's growth transformed it into a full-blown organization, one that would focus on other threatened wildlife and ultimately encompass other regions of Brazil. The husband-and-wife team decided to create the Instituto de Pesquisas Ecológicas (the Institute of Ecological Studies), IPE for short. That decision brought Claudio to my home in the suburbs of Philadelphia. We sat down at the kitchen table for lunch and he put forth his plan.

"Bill, Suzana and I think we'll need about $20,000 in seed money to get IPE off the ground. I'd like to ask Hope and Bob for half of the start-up costs. What do you think?" Claudio was referring to Hope and Bob Stevens, mutual friends in Montana who ran the Fanwood Foundation. Hope had been able to spend time at Claudio and Suzana's field station during trips to Brazil to visit her sister. Hope and Bob also hosted Claudio and me at their home in Bozeman, Montana, inviting us to lecture at nearby Montana State University, where we spoke about Brazil's urgent primate and tropical forest conservation issues.

I thought for a moment. "Why not ask them for *all* of it, not just half? They love what you and Suzana are doing and their foundation can easily afford a grant of that size. I'd ask them to fund the start-up costs in full."

And so he did. Claudio got on the phone right there and then, and made the case for creating IPE. I don't think we had finished our sandwiches and I didn't even have to eavesdrop on the conversation to know what their answer was. Claudio enthusiastically thanked them, *"Muito obrigado,"* hung up the phone, turned to me and smiled.

I beat him to the punch. "See, I told you they'd want to get you guys up and running."

He nodded. "They said they were honored to be asked and proud to help."

Since that auspicious day, IPE has blossomed into one of the most energetic and productive of Brazil's conservation organizations. For three decades, IPE researchers have helped restore degraded forests, launched environmental education campaigns and supported many ecologically sustainable businesses. Their work continues.

In 2002,

Time Magazine recognized Claudio and Suzana as Heroes of the Planet, spotlighting their accomplishments and those of their colleagues at IPE. From relatively modest beginnings focused on the black lion tamarins of Morro do Diabo, the organization has expanded its activities to include missions to help save creatures such as manatees in the Amazon (the world's largest tropical wilderness), and tapirs and jaguars in the Pantanal (the world's largest wetland).

III. GOLDEN LION TAMARIN

Toward the end of my first trip to Brazil, two former Peace Corps volunteers arrived in Rio de Janeiro. Armed with a grant from the Smithsonian, Jim and Lou Ann Dietz planned to spend the next two years at the Poço das Antas Biological Reserve studying golden lion tamarins. What they didn't count on was being hassled big time by airport officials who claimed their papers were not in order, and they certainly didn't expect to be threatened with deportation if they didn't take the requisite medical exams on the spot. Their situation was both inconvenient and irritating, but discretion prevailed. The Dietzes consented to re-examination, were permitted entry and afterward joined Russ and me for dinner. We even ordered a cake to celebrate Jim's 35th birthday.

Between 1983 and 2000, the Smithsonian National Zoological Park and the Rio de Janeiro Primate Center reintroduced nearly 150 captive-born golden lion tamarins to the wild. Unfortunately, less than a third of these animals survived more than two years, succumbing to predators, disease, snakebite and other factors. Fortunately, nearly three-quarters of the offspring born to the survivors lived at least two years, which more than doubled the reintroduced population by the year 2000.

The golden lion tamarin is the best known of all the lion tamarins and, I would argue, the most attractive. But, as has been true for its cousins, this species has suffered dramatic declines due to the loss of its forest habitat and the impact of an unregulated pet trade. The one spot in the world in which it lives is the state of Rio de Janeiro. Dr. Coimbra-Filho, Dr. Devra Kleiman of the Smithsonian Institution, and Russ were largely responsible for bringing this tiny primate's plight to the world's attention and

GOLDEN LION TAMARIN, THE HOUSTON ZOO, 2005

initiating efforts to ensure its survival, including its protection at Poço das Antas.

Pretty much all that awaited the Dietzes at the Reserve was a dilapidated hut—the ultimate fixer-upper and their home for the next two years. At least a hundred bats roosted in the rafters, each one contributing its share of smelly deposits to the guano-covered floor. But Jim and Lou Ann were young, determined and confident that their new abode would be spick-and-span in no time at all.

Today, the two most serious threats facing golden lion tamarins are yellow fever epidemics and hybridization with pet golden-headed lion tamarins that have been released into forests around Rio de Janeiro. Researchers believe a yellow fever outbreak reduced golden lion tamarin numbers in Poço das Antas by more than 80 percent. Meanwhile, efforts are ongoing to capture released pet golden-headed lion tamarins to minimize the threat of hybridization between the two species.

LESSON LEARNED:
Every endangered species needs a champion or champions, individuals who dedicate themselves to ensuring that creature's survival.

FREE-RANGING GOLDEN LION TAMARIN, THE HOUSTON ZOO, 2004

APRIL, THE TAPIR, THE BELIZE ZOO, 1986

MEET
MISS APRIL

Tapirs are special!
We're the symbol of our nation!
So make sure we're here for
Our future generation!

Tapir Exhibit Graphic, Belize Zoo and Tropical Education Center

You're about to meet a very special animal at a very special zoo created by a very special woman. However, I'm obliged to first inject a bit of background that explains how we've arrived at this point, so I thank you in advance for your patience.

A couple of years after my muriqui presentation at the zoo conference in Vancouver, British Columbia, Wildlife Preservation Trust International (WPTI) invited me to apply for its executive director's position. Long story short, Russ gave me his blessing and encouraged me to apply. The interview went well and the Konstant family left New York and headed for Pennsylvania.

WPTI was a sister organization to the Jersey Wildlife Preservation Trust, based at the Jersey Zoo on the English Channel island of the same name. Renowned British author and naturalist Gerald Durrell founded the two organizations and although not quite a household name here in the United States, his books were required reading for generations of English schoolchildren. The nature tales of his youth highlighted in two popular television series, *My Family and Other Animals* and *The Durrells in Corfu*, continue to have broad international appeal.

Despite WPTI's board of directors offering me the job, the founder's blessing was also required before I officially took the reins. I met Gerald Durrell and his wife, Lee, on a flight to Charleston, South Carolina, where WPTI was holding its annual board meeting. Seated three across at 30,000 feet, Gerry, Lee and I spoke about the intricacies and challenges of coordinating our two organizations' programs across the pond. In the hour and 40 minutes from takeoff to touchdown, my new mentor expertly laid out the road map for what would lie ahead.

MAILGRAM SERVICE CENTER
MIDDLETOWN, VA, 22645
07AM

Western Union **Mailgram**

1-091016G038 02/07/86 ICS IPMIIHX IISS PHAA
KNY847 1949PHIL GBBM BIRMINGHAM 50 07 1428

BILL KONSTANT
WILDLIFE PRESERVATION TRUST INTERNATIONAL
34 STREET GIRARD AVENUE
PHILADELPHIA
PA 19104

YOU WILL NOW BE KONSTANTLY IN OUR THOUGHTS, KONSTANTLY
AT OUR BECK AND CALL, KONSTANTLY OUR GUIDE, MENTOR AND FRIEND, AND
A KONSTANT SOURCE OF ADVICE AND HELP BUT, SO PEOPLE WON'T KNOW
THIS, WE WILL CALL YOU BILL. WELCOME ON BOARD THE ARK.

THE DURRELLS AND EVERYONE IN JERSEY
JERSEY
UNITED KINGDOM
07 FEBRUARY 1986

NNN

09:32 EST

MGMCOMP

Gerry graciously accepted the unofficial title bestowed upon him: The Champion of the Uglies. By "uglies," his followers meant those often small, innocuous and obscure creatures that deserve our help and perhaps could do with better press agents. Gerry had given refuge to a number of them at his zoo

GERALD DURRELL AND A LESSER HEDGEHOG TENREC, JERSEY ZOO
PHOTO COURTESY OF ROBERT RATTNER

in Jersey—many were part of captive breeding programs set up to ensure their species' survival in the wild. Among the uglies were fruit-eating bats and insect-eating lizards from a handful of Indian Ocean islands, ghost-like lemurs from Madagascar, and seemingly lowly land snails from French Polynesia in the western Pacific. These threatened species and many more would dominate my "conservation calendar" during the late 1980s and set the stage for many 21st-century animal adventures.

A few years after our flight to Charleston, Gerry, Lee and I found ourselves together again on a trip. This time it was in a rental car en route from Washington, DC north to Rhode Island. The Roger Williams Park Zoo in Providence was the first stop on a multi-city string of speaking engagements. I was driving and Lee sat up front while Gerry enjoyed a late morning catnap in the back seat. We had reached New Jersey, driving along Route 1.

"Oh, shit!" That's my go-to exclamation when things begin heading south in a hurry. It's an expression of absolutely no use in an emergency, save for conveying some sense of urgency, and it was the best I could muster as the front grill of an 18-wheeler began bearing down on us from behind.

"What's wrong, Bill?" Lee could see that my eyes were laser-focused on the rearview mirror.

"We're gonna get hit!" Our car was in the right-hand lane, moving in sync with traffic. The large truck behind us had been in the left lane but began veering right and accelerating toward us. I can only assume that the driver had fallen asleep at the wheel. A car was directly in front of us and another was to our left. We were boxed in and plumb outta luck. The truck's grill filled the rearview mirror when its front bumper slammed into us.

"Here we go!" My fingers tightened on the steering wheel. Because the truck was moving diagonally across lanes, the contact drove our car toward the shoulder. The impact must have awakened the truck driver, who then hit the brakes in pure reflex. This was real-life bumper cars at 60 miles an hour, and now I can honestly say that I know how the eight ball feels when the cue ball sends it careening across the pool table. It was all I could do to steer into the skid and keep from flipping over or being driven into the ditch. I heard Gerry begin to stir in the back seat.

"Hold on!" Our car remained on the roadway, but its rear end was moving forward faster than its front, twirling us perpendicular to traffic as we skidded to a precarious stop. I glanced out the driver's side window, once again looking directly into the front end of the big rig. The truck rammed us a second time, leaving less than 12 inches of door between my left shoulder and an enormous front bumper and grill. The collision drove us a few dozen yards farther down the road. Somehow, miraculously, the vehicles behind us were able to steer clear of the crash.

Lee, Gerry and I were shaken, but none of us were hurt. I tried my door, crumpled somewhat but still functional. Stepping out onto the highway to assess the damage, I was flabbergasted. It actually didn't look all that bad. In fact, it turned out that the car was still drivable, at least enough to get us off the highway and out of any additional danger. The truck driver had pulled off the roadway and walked toward us. English was his second language, which added a slight degree of difficulty to the conversation, but it was clear he was prepared to deny any fault. After a few minutes, a patrol car pulled up, an officer stepped out and began taking our statements.

"Gerald Dur-RELL? Did you say your name is Gerald Dur-RELL?" The officer pronounced Gerry's surname the way many Americans do, stressing the second syllable.

"Yes, Gerald Durrell, that would be me." I'm guessing that Gerry never stopped being annoyed by this mispronunciation. At the same time, I think he also got some enjoyment imitating it, which he could do perfectly. He refrained this time so as not to offend the officer, who didn't appear to notice the difference.

"I'm a big fan of yours," the officer confessed. "I've read all of your books. I especially like your stories about growing up in Greece. You had the best childhood anyone could have had!" Now, can somebody please tell me what the chances are that a New Jersey cop would be a Gerald Durrell groupie? But it gets even better.

The police reports required some additional paperwork, so we decided to clear the accident scene, drive down the road just a bit and finish the formalities over lunch at a local diner. Our new policeman buddy joined us. The conversation quickly drifted from details of the crash to everyone's favorite animal. The officer's favorite just happened to be the tapir. Tapirs are somewhat smaller cousins of rhinos, horses, zebras and the like.

CENTRAL AMERICAN TAPIR WITH CALF, VILLA GRISELDA, PANAMA, 2005

Gerry, of course, had numerous stories about tapirs, several of which he rattled off over lunch for our entertainment. His tales were the best medicine for the anxiety of our roller coaster, topsy-turvy day.

Reminiscing about the adventure years later, Lee reminded me that, just as the conversation wound down, the policeman received a call regarding another crash just down the road. As he rushed for the door, his parting words were "Oh shit, here we go again!"

Like Gerry, I had a tapir story of my own, one from a small, English-speaking country in Central America. Belize Zoo director Sharon Matola opened the gate to the tapir enclosure and motioned for me to enter. The resident, April, was a vibrant young female in excellent condition, despite having arrived at the Zoo suffering from a severe screwworm infection several years earlier. April had seen me coming from the other end of her exhibit: a large, fenced-in patch of rain forest. She wasted no time in her approach, sensing that I was the bearer of some tasty treats, in this case, a handful of carrots.

146

APRIL THE TAPIR, THE BELIZE ZOO, 1989

April stopped a couple of feet in front of me, at which point she reached up with her long flexible snout to inspect what I had to offer. That gave me a glimpse of her impressive dentition. For an instant, a memory of what I'd read as a child in Frank Buck's *Bring 'Em Back Alive* flashed in my head. An adult Malay tapir that the famous animal collector was trying to medicate suddenly charged him, knocked him down and began dragging him around its pen. I remembered an artist's drawing of the incident that depicted what looked like a crazed beast, teeth bared, apparently intent on ripping off Buck's face. As he told the story, only the sudden arrival of his indigenous helpers saved his life.

Four tapir species exist worldwide, three in the New World tropics and one in Southeast Asia. April was a Central American tapir, named for the month in which she arrived at the Belize

147

MAYA THE JAGUAR, THE BELIZE ZOO, 1991
PHOTO COURTESY OF TED WOOD

Zoo. Central American tapirs range from southern Mexico to Colombia. The Brazilian tapir lives throughout much of South America. The mountain tapir, a resident of the high Andes, is found only in Colombia, Ecuador and Peru. The Malay tapir is literally a distant relative, found only in the Asian countries of Indonesia, Malaysia, Myanmar and Thailand.

Tapirs are relatively large, robust mammals. All four species stand at least three feet tall at the shoulder and can weigh as much as a quarter of a ton. The three New World species are brown, while the Malay tapir's body is half black and half white. Remarkably enough, the young of all four species appear nearly identical: a brownish-black coat with white stripes and spots, looking very much like four-legged watermelons. In appearance, tapirs more closely resemble pigs or peccaries than their closest relatives, horses and rhinos.

Rivers, lakes and swamps are common features of tapir habitat, and plant matter—leaves, twigs and fruits—comprises 100

SHARON MATOLA AND APRIL, THE BELIZE ZOO, 1991
PHOTO COURTESY OF TED WOOD

percent of their diet. Habitat loss and hunting threaten all tapirs. They're the largest mammals in Central and South America and as such, they offer hunters a veritable feast for the price of a shotgun shell. Aside from humans, the jaguar, the largest Neotropical carnivore, is the tapir's most significant predator.

The scent of carrots told April that I could be trusted. I was well acquainted with the capabilities of an elephant's trunk, a spider monkey's tail and a giraffe's tongue, but hadn't anticipated similar dexterity from a tapir's snout. With the flip of her upper lip and a quick twist of her long tongue, April snatched a carrot from my hand, deftly inserted it into her mouth and began to chomp away. I recalled the graphic prominently displayed in front of April's enclosure. A chalked message on the blackboard sign displayed a myth believed by many Belizeans about the animal most know as the mountain cow. Legend has it that a tapir can and will skin a person alive with its flexible snout.

"April is very well-behaved," Sharon assured me. "She won't skin you alive," Sharon paused then wryly added, "as long as you keep feeding her."

I chuckled, thinking back to the day that Sharon and I had met. It was at another of those zoo conferences, this one in Miami in 1984. Nan had come along this time. We had split up to attend different presentations based on our animal interests, agreeing that we'd meet in the lobby before having lunch. As soon as she saw me, she grabbed me by the arm. "Buzz, you have to meet someone." Buzz is Nan's pet name for me. Just to be clear, it's short for Buzzard, not Buzz Lightyear. "She's from Belize and she's just told me all about her zoo. You need to hear her story." Nan led me by the hand through the crowd to a tall woman wearing a jumpsuit and a jaguar-spotted bandana. She was holding a large photo album. Sharon's tanned face and chiseled features told me that she had spent serious time in the tropics living close to nature.

Sharon, Nan and I spent the next hour or so poring over her photos of Central American wildlife: jaguars, pumas, ocelots, margays, tapirs, kinkajous, scarlet macaws, toucans, crocodiles, spider monkeys, howler monkeys and more. All of them, Sharon explained, had been featured in a recent documentary about the tropical forests and creatures of Belize. She had been hired to train and care for the animal actors and was on a first-name basis with April the Tapir, Maya the Jaguar and Rambo the Toucan.

When the film project wrapped and funding for the animals' care ran out, Sharon was given the job of finding suitable homes for the cast. The powers that be suggested that she simply set them free in the jungle, which would have been nothing more than a death sentence. Instead, the young biologist and Baltimore native decided that Belize needed a national zoo—a place where Belizeans could learn about their precious native wildlife. And so the Belize Zoo and Tropical Education Center was born, a

RAMBO THE TOUCAN, THE BELIZE ZOO, 1991
PHOTO COURTESY OF TED WOOD

jungle menagerie with no budget at the time other than Sharon's own savings and pocket money. In its nascent days, the Zoo was a conglomeration of make-shift enclosures held together with welded wire, hog nails, hand-sawn lumber and a whole lotta love. What the animals' homes may have lacked in design, they more than made up for in natural habitat and space.

I was impressed. It was impossible not to be. "Sharon, I'd like you to prepare a proposal requesting a grant for the construction of a spider monkey or howler monkey exhibit at your zoo." I was still working for the World Wildlife Fund-US with Russ, and the two of us comanaged the Primate Action Fund, which awarded grants ranging from $1,000 to $3,000. That would have been enough to begin work on a proper exhibit for one of these two primates. "Make sure that you emphasize the need to educate the children of Belize regarding their national wildlife heritage." Sharon was deeply committed to reaching every child in the country, inviting them to her zoo or bringing some of the animal ambassadors to their villages if they couldn't make the trip.

Thus began a friendship that would span nearly 40 years.

A few years into our collaboration, a producer by the name of Bev Aaron from WPVI-TV in Philadelphia learned about the Belize Zoo project and proposed shooting a feature for the station's weekly *Prime Time* program. He and his assistant, Al Rodriguez, invited me to help tell Sharon's story. Our adventure began with a dusty, 30-mile drive along the Hummingbird Highway from the Belize City airport to the Zoo. Filming, of course, couldn't begin until the crew had its obligatory audience with April the Tapir. After all, the tapir is the national animal of Belize. We then joined families who were strolling the grounds, encountering the rest of Belize's animal ambassadors and soaking in their messages handwritten in chalk on the blackboard exhibit signs, which spoke directly to visitors. The crocodiles admonished people who throw rocks at them in the wild: "Please let me lie here peacefully! Admire my form! My skin! And my size!" The scarlet macaws boasted about their natural beauty and lamented their rarity: "We're very red and very rare! We macaw parrots are as scarce in the region as a rice and beans dinner on the North Pole!"

The narrator opened the television show by saying, "There is laughter here and wonder." Sharon told the story of one of her first visitors, an old man who had traveled for hours by bus. "When I started to tell him about the natural history of these animals, that they did live in Belize, that they still lived in healthy populations …" Sharon paused, clearly impacted by the moment. "He just started to cry right in front of me. I was taken aback and asked him what was wrong, and he looked me in the eye, tears pouring down his face, and he said, 'I'm really sorry miss, but I've lived in Belize my whole life and this is the first time I've ever seen the animals of my country.' And I can really say that my life changed at that point."

The documentary also highlighted a local tour operator visiting the Zoo with his wife. He spoke highly of Sharon's efforts and their impact on his country's growing conservation ethic. "She has given a lot of her life to this Zoo and it's shown the work she's put into it. It's great! Belizeans are beginning to appreciate it, and we've gone by leaps and bounds beyond many countries in establishing conservation laws."

With some seed money in hand, Sharon and I launched a much more ambitious fundraising effort, reaching out first to some of her friends, including actor Harrison Ford. Sharon had worked with Ford some years before while he was in Belize shooting the movie *The Mosquito Coast*. He had visited the Zoo in its early days and responded to her request with a generous gift for the construction project.

I brought our mission to Gerald Durrell's attention at a board meeting on the Isle of Jersey. Gerry was supportive from the start—remember the special place he had in his heart for tapirs—but he was concerned that a project of this magnitude might consume me. I assured him that wouldn't happen and that none of my other commitments would suffer. Seated next to me on the dais, Gerry leaned forward, his chin lightly resting on his two hands as they gripped the top of his walking stick. He cocked his head and asked me, "And just what is it,

The new and improved Belize Zoo and Tropical Education Center opened in 1991 after an overhaul that required several years. Its exhibits are embedded in the surrounding forests and savannas—wonderful for the residents and for visitors who get to see animals living in their natural habitats. The Zoo is a prominent force for nature conservation in Belize, as well as a partner with neighboring nations in efforts to create wildlife corridors across international borders.

my enthusiastic young friend, that assures you this dynamic young woman and her tropical menagerie are worthy of such investment?"

I responded without hesitation, leaning forward just as he had done. "Because, Gerry, if you were in Belize today, *you* would *be* Sharon Matola." Chuckles from the crowd nearly drowned out his mock protestation to the implied question of gender in my remark. I seem to remember him vigorously tapping his cane on the floor and calling the room to order. He then smiled and nodded his approval, opening the way to the next agenda item.

A few months later, I was invited to speak at a New York City event called Don't Bungle the Jungle. It was the brainchild of Companions of Art and Nature, a small organization based in Red Hook, New York. In preparation, cofounders Marie-Pierre Astier, her husband, Mikhail Mesh, and iconic painter and street artist Kenny Scharf had invited several wildlife conservationists, including Russ and me, to speak to an audience of artists. Russ kicked off the presentations, speaking about the need to save primates and their tropical forest habitats. He was followed by Mark Plotkin, an ethnobotanist and colleague at Conservation International, who spoke about the need to safeguard the botanical knowledge of Amerindian tribes. I followed with a talk about the new Belize Zoo and a future for threatened Central American wildlife.

A Spanish artist hosted our presentations at his home, the entire floor of an old New York brownstone. A single step out of the elevator and you were in his living room. After a cocktail reception, everyone took their seats among the rows of folding chairs in an adjoining room. I sat along the center aisle in the second row. A petite Asian woman with short black hair stopped and eyed the empty space next to mine. "Is that seat taken?"

"No," I answered, standing up and politely motioning toward the seat. "It's yours."

She sat down, placed her purse below the seat and scanned the room for people she might know. Then she turned in my direction and reached out her hand. "Hello, I'm Yoko." Yep, that Yoko.

Don't Bungle the Jungle was a star-studded affair, spanning a number of venues. It also featured a concert at the Brooklyn Academy of Music. Madonna and Sandra Bernhard cohosted the concert, which included performances by The B-52s and Bob Weir of the Grateful Dead. The event raised hundreds of thousands of dollars, which helped Sharon's zoo-building efforts enormously.

Construction required several years, including completion of a beautiful visitor center dedicated to Gerry Durrell, who wrote:

> The charm of the Belize Zoo has worked its magic on children and adults alike, and they flock there to look at the wonderful animals that inhabit their country, most of which they have never seen. Sharon was determined to give both the animals and people of Belize a proper zoo. So, with courage and charm combined with a certain Machiavellian cunning, she got the government to set aside a section of land, and by fundraising everywhere she could (no donation was too small), she raised the money to build the new zoo ... Sharon Matola ... is a very remarkable person indeed.

A children's book titled *Hoodwink the Owl* has a special place on my living room shelf. Sharon wrote it and signed the copy for my children. Hoodwink was a wise, old spectacled owl, the color of chocolate, with pretty white rings around his eyes. Hoodwink flew all over Belize watching howler monkeys playing in the

SHARON MATOLA AND A BABY TAPIR, THE BELIZE ZOO, 1991
PHOTO COURTESY OF TED WOOD

fig trees, manatees swimming in the sea, and jaguars prowling the forest on moonlit nights. Sharon wrote two more books for young people about the wildlife of Central America. Reading her books, the children of Belize have not only learned about their animal neighbors but how important the tropical forests, marshes, rivers and coral reefs are to their survival.

Soon after April the Tapir's arrival at Sharon's zoo in 1983, Belize designated April 27th as National Tapir Day. Since 2008, people worldwide have celebrated that date as World Tapir Day. In 2013, April the Tapir passed away at the age of 30. She was the oldest known tapir at the time, and her memory and her impact live on.

Sharon Matola tragically passed away at the age of 66 from a sudden heart attack in March 2021. A few months before, we had been emailing about the impact of COVID-19 in Belize. She mentioned that the only time she removed her mask was when feeding her pet harpy eagle. I also was able to lend a small hand in her effort to purchase 1,000 acres of tropical savanna that adjoined the Zoo—excellent habitat for jaguars, tapirs and a variety of Belizean birds. I'm pleased that Sharon lived to see that campaign completed.

LESSON LEARNED:
Individual animals can serve as icons for their species and can become especially powerful symbols when they team up with humans who understand how special they are—humans who seem to run on jet fuel.

RING-TAILED LEMURS, SYMBOLS OF MADAGASCAR, 2016

THE GHOSTS
OF
MADAGASCAR

*A man in a movie theater notices what looks like
a lemur sitting next to him.
Surprised, he asks, "Are you a lemur?"
"Yes."
"What are you doing at the movies?"
"Well, I liked the book."*

Unknown Origin

It was June 2002. About 30 minutes into our trek, we came to rest on a low rise. I peered out over a patchwork of dry forest and savanna. Half a dozen zebu cattle stood along a hillside to the west, returning our stares as they chewed the sparse vegetation that somehow manages to draw sufficient nutrients from the red clay soil. The zebu originated in India; also known as Brahman, they have a distinctive hump on their upper back. The curvature of the zebus' horns matched the outline of their ribs, attesting to the meager amounts of protein and carbohydrates making their way up the food chain. Our viewpoint was on the outskirts of Daraina, a community of approximately 10,000 people in a remote northern corner of Madagascar. The nearest patch of tropical dry forest was another half-hour's walk through open hill country.

Directly ahead, along the ridgeline, I could make out what looked like giant balls of cotton in the sparsely-leaved treetops.

PACHYPODIUM IN BLOOM, NORTHEASTERN MADAGASCAR, 1998

Earlier, one of my companions, a Malagasy botanist, explained that a number of the native trees produce magnificent white flower clusters. I pulled the binoculars from my pack and trained them on one of the more impressive clusters. Suddenly, it rocketed five or six feet onto the branch of another tree. Since when do flowers jump?

GOLDEN-CROWNED SIFAKA, MADAGASCAR'S DARAINA REGION, 1998

What lay ahead for us that morning was one of Madagascar's unique animal treasures, the golden-crowned sifaka (pronounced shee-FAHK-uh). This large lemur's vanilla coat contrasts with a jet-black face and Halloween-orange eyes—a striking combination highlighted by a golden crown of fur atop its head. The species was unknown until 1974 when it was first spotted by British anthropologist Ian Tattersall of the American Museum of Natural History. Fourteen years later, Ian described *Propithecus tattersalli*, still referred to as Tattersall's sifaka by many of his colleagues.

Like Madagascar's eight other sifakas, this one is a "vertical clinger and leaper," a term that describes how these large lemurs move through their forest habitats. Travel begins from a resting position, the animal's body upright and often propped against a tree trunk. With its elbows and knees flexed, and both hands and feet clinging to the vertical support, the lemur launches itself into the air. Even mothers with youngsters embracing their bellies rocket through the forest this way—*boing-boing-boinging* from one tree trunk or branch to the next.

The name

"lemur" comes from the Latin *lemure*, which may be translated as "ghost," "spirit" or "specter" from the days of ancient Rome. Carl Linnaeus, the father of binomial nomenclature, gave lemurs their Latin names in the 1750s, perhaps because many of these Madagascar endemics are nocturnal creatures.

The first time I set foot in Madagascar was in 1988. I was leading a group of about 10 people—all members of Wildlife Preservation Trust International. WPTI supported a handful of conservation projects on the island, and the members wanted to see the results of their support firsthand. In 2000, I returned with Conservation International to begin work on either a new nature reserve or national park. Here in Daraina, I worked closely with Serge Rajaobelina, the founder of Fanamby, a nongovernmental organization devoted to preserving Madagascar's unique biological diversity.

Two years later, I headed back to Madagascar to check on the project's progress. The country's Daraina region cried out for conservation action. Much of its forests had already been cut, the wood collected for charcoal, and the land cultivated for crops or turned over to the anemic-looking cattle that became part of the landscape. Adding insult to injury, Daraina's dry river beds had been gouged by itinerant miners who sought gold and precious gems that might lay hidden beneath. Curiously enough, the human intruders paid little attention to the sifakas. They didn't hunt them or take them as pets. On the contrary, many miners even befriended and fed the inquisitive animals, which helped set the stage for successful conservation initiatives and ensure this endangered species' survival.

Spanish biologist Astrid Vargas also played a major role in Fanamby's efforts to save the golden-crowned sifaka. She invited me to visit the field station she and her team had built.

NORTHEASTERN MADAGASCAR'S DARAINA REGION, 1998

I met Astrid back in the late 1980s in the United States, where she helped reintroduce captive-born, black-footed ferrets to the wild. In Madagascar, we spent several days hiking through the northern hills, meeting the local people and gauging their enthusiasm for a protected area in their own backyard. It took a number of years to build the support necessary for a successful project.

In 2005, with support from Conservation International, Fanamby established the Loky Manambato protected area of close to 50,000 acres, encompassing the core of the golden-crowned sifaka's range. Today, Malagasy and international tourists alike can travel to Daraina to observe this endangered lemur and many other native species in their natural habitats.

Lemur diversity is nothing short of remarkable. More than 100 living species and subspecies are known to science, all of them endemic to Madagascar. Smallest among these unique primates are the nocturnal mouse, dwarf and fork-marked lemurs. Madame Berthe's mouse lemur, in fact, is the world's smallest

The ring-tailed lemur, known by its local name of *maki*, is emblematic of Madagascar. The best known of all the island's animals, it was the first species to greet me on my inaugural trip to that island nation off the coast of Southern Africa in the Indian Ocean. A resident of southern Madagascar's dry forest regions, it is endangered by ongoing habitat loss, hunting for bushmeat and live capture for pets.

primate, weighing little more than an ounce. There are beetles that weigh three times as much! The largest group of these primates is known as "true lemurs"; they include the ring-tailed, bamboo, brown, white-fronted, collared, black, red-bellied, crowned, mongoose, black-and-white ruffed, and red ruffed lemurs. Most are either diurnal or cathemeral (equally active day or night).

The family Indriidae includes the woolly lemurs and the largest of Madagascar's primates, the sifakas and the indri (an arboreal, essentially tailless look-a-like known for its long mournful songs that conjure images of restless spirits).

Sitting in a family of its own is the aye-aye (pronounced eye-eye), the world's largest nocturnal primate. Eighteenth-century scientists were uncertain of its taxonomic status, some believing the creature to be some bizarre type of squirrel. I chuckle at Gerald Durrell's description: "... like a witch's cat conceived by Walt Disney, with a huge bushy tail like a flue brush and enormous eyes."

Not all of Gerry's writings about the aye-aye were so amusing, such as this scathing letter he wrote to me many years ago (the sensitive parts redacted). It is, however, one I will always treasure. As you can see from the tiny snippet—the top of the first page of a three-page tirade—the grand old man chewed me out right from the get-go, and it didn't get much prettier for the remaining two pages. The story is complicated, but suffice it to

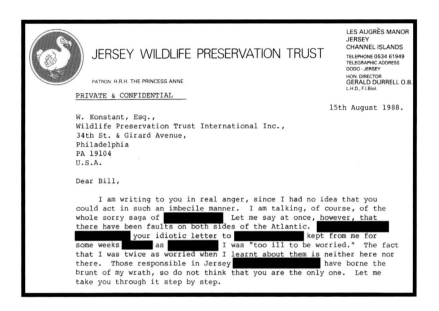

JERSEY WILDLIFE PRESERVATION TRUST

LES AUGRÈS MANOR
JERSEY
CHANNEL ISLANDS
TELEPHONE 0534 61949
TELEGRAPHIC ADDRESS
DODO · JERSEY
HON. DIRECTOR
GERALD DURRELL O.B.
L.H.D., F.I.Biol.

PRIVATE & CONFIDENTIAL

15th August 1988.

W. Konstant, Esq.,
Wildlife Preservation Trust International Inc.,
34th St. & Girard Avenue,
Philadelphia
PA 19104
U.S.A.

Dear Bill,

I am writing to you in real anger, since I had no idea that you could act in such an imbecile manner. I am talking, of course, of the whole sorry saga of ▮▮▮▮▮▮▮▮ Let me say at once, however, that there have been faults on both sides of the Atlantic. ▮▮▮▮▮▮▮ ▮▮▮▮▮▮ your idiotic letter to ▮▮▮▮▮▮▮ kept from me for some weeks ▮▮▮▮ as ▮▮▮▮▮▮▮ I was "too ill to be worried." The fact that I was twice as worried when I learnt about them is neither here nor there. Those responsible in Jersey ▮▮▮▮▮▮▮▮ have borne the brunt of my wrath, so do not think that you are the only one. Let me take you through it step by step.

say that Gerry was angry—angry that I had approved funding for an aye-aye project that he felt wasn't worthy of support. The aye-aye was one of the "uglies" that he was fully committed to saving, and I had made a decision of which he didn't approve.

The problem was that Gerry had copied this letter to all the members of WPTI's executive committee, one of whom called and tried his best to persuade me not to respond. That might have been good advice for someone else, but I decided otherwise. Gerry's three-page thrashing of me was met with a four-page retaliation of my own, peppered with what I felt was sufficient humor to diffuse any meaningful feud. I then filed both our letters away for future reminiscence over a glass or two of wine, but the subject never again arose. A bit of background here might help explain the chain of events that followed our little clash.

Aye-ayes are secretive creatures by nature and rarely seen by people, which likely contributed to the mistaken belief by some

AYE-AYE, DUKE LEMUR CENTER, DUKE UNIVERSITY, NORTH CAROLINA, 2007

scientists that the species had vanished sometime during the middle of the 20th century. For decades, when villagers would encounter aye-ayes, it wasn't at all unusual for the animals to be killed on sight. Moreover, the aye-aye looks positively devilish, so many Malagasy believe that it's an evil spirit or a harbinger of bad luck. Its bat-like ears, bulging eyes, and long skeletal fingers combine to give it a ghoulish appearance, as well as an image problem that's hard to shake.

Field surveys launched during the 1980s began to document the presence of aye-ayes in scattered locations throughout Madagascar. The species was much more widespread than originally thought, but nowhere was it found in large numbers. Gerry felt that a handful could be captured and brought to the Jersey Zoo for breeding, creating an insurance colony as a hedge against the species' possible extinction. Such was his plan for the species' survival, which wasn't in conflict with the now disputed project I had funded, but perhaps he considered my actions as competition. Fair enough if that's what Gerry thought, but it just wasn't the case.

INDRI
ARTWORK COURTESY OF STEPHEN NASH

In fact, I was 100 percent behind his idea for an expedition to help save the aye-aye. So was one of my Philadelphia-based board members, Marilyn Steinbright, and her longtime friend, Harvey Miller, who together offered to host a donor's luncheon to finance Gerry's aye-aye rescue efforts. The luncheon setting was perfect and the turnout was huge. Unfortunately, Gerry fell sick and was unable to travel, so Lee flew in to save the day and woo the crowd. The event raised more than $40,000 for the Madagascar expedition chronicled in Gerry's last book, *The Aye-Aye and I*. Six aye-ayes were brought from the island of Madagascar to the English Channel island of Jersey, where a breeding colony was established. The book also tells of bringing back several Lake Alaotra bamboo lemurs—the only primate known to live in and feed on papyrus—as well as specimens of the equally threatened flat-backed spider tortoise (*kapidola* in Malagasy) and the Malagasy giant jumping rat. A quarter of a century later, all these species remain conservation priorities for the Durrell Wildlife Conservation Trust as well as a number of other international organizations.

To date, a handful of lemur species have been the focus of documented introduction or reintroduction projects. In 1967, biologists captured aye-ayes from coastal villages on the mainland and released them on the offshore island of Nosy Mangabe in the Bay of Antongil. Between 1997 and 2001, the Madagascar Fauna Group released 13 captive-born black-and-white ruffed lemurs to the Betampona Nature Reserve, reinforcing the protected area's existing population. In 2006, the Madagascar Biodiversity and Biogeography Project (a collaboration of Omaha's Henry Doorly Zoo, Madagascar National Parks and the national Ministry of the Environment, Forestry and Tourism) translocated wild-born diademed sifakas and black-and-white ruffed lemurs to the Analazamaotra Special Reserve, where hunting had eliminated both species. The reintroduced populations are now, thankfully, protected.

LESSON LEARNED:

When you find yourself on the opposite side of an issue with a colleague, don't be afraid to speak truth to power. Then get back to tackling the important tasks at hand, because chances are that you're both fighting for the same cause.

MALAGASY WOMEN AND CHILDREN OF THE DARAINA REGION, 1998

MALAGASY FAMILY, NORTHERN MADAGASCAR, 1998

Bill Konstant

Alexander Peal

October 16, 1990

Dear Bill:

Three weeks ago we heard a rumor that Alexander Peal had been executed along with 28 other government officials by the rebel forces in Liberia. This set off a chain of events to find out if it was actually true.

We ascertained that a Liberian refugee contacted Emily Peal (Alex's wife who had reached France on one of the last flights out of Monrovia) telling her that Alex was alive and in the Soul Clinic refugee camp. Alex had given this refugee (a friend) the last of his money to ensure safe passage for the man.

After much effort on our part, on Tuesday, October 9, a rebel leader sent a vehicle to find Alex and bring him to the rebel base camp. Alex was then able to phone from the base camp's satellite phone and assure me that he and his children were okay; however, he had no way to leave Liberia. I had some conversations with the rebel leaders and asked if they would give Alex safe passage to the Ivory Coast border, pointing out that Alex was important for international relations. I was assured that no harm would come to Alex and that he would be personally escorted in a convoy to the border. This was done.

On Friday, October 12, Alex reached the Ivory Coast border with his small children. On Sunday, October 14, after a long bus ride Alex reached Abidjan, the capitol of the Ivory Coast, and was able to call me.

Alex gave me news about the situation in Liberia. For instance, the animals at the Monrovia zoo, the animal orphanage, and the chimps on the islands have been killed for food. Most of the rangers of Sapo National Park are okay, but disbanded, and all the vehicles and equipment have been taken by government troops. Some of the people who worked at Forestry Development Authority were killed when they took refuge at the Payneville headquarters when fighting broke out there.

Right now Alex has no money. We need funds to cover his expenses in Ivory Coast and to fly him and his children to France where they can be cared for until the war ends in Liberia.

We have worked hard to find and ensure the safety of Alex Peal. Along with many other conservation organizations, we believe he is essential to Liberia's future, when the country can begin rebuilding its wildlife and national parks system.

Sincerely

WILDLIFE
AND
WAR

The elephant never gets tired of carrying its tusks.

Liberian Proverb

I met Alex Peal at the Jersey Zoo's International Training Center in 1986, several years before receiving this gut-punch of a letter. It was a call to action which I knew I had to share with our members in WPTI's newsletter, *On the Edge*. Alex was Liberia's director for wildlife and national parks at the time, even though the first national park in this small West African nation did not yet exist. He was also the president of the Society for the Conservation of Nature of Liberia (SCNL). While on the island of Jersey, Alex worked with a number of endangered species and began writing his country's wildlife laws. All the while, his homeland was hurtling headlong into civil war.

Liberia sits just north of the Equator on Africa's Atlantic coast. The extent of tropical forest in the country is impressive—the largest remaining expanse, in fact, in all of West Africa. Incredibly rich in wildlife, these forests harbor well-known species such as forest elephants and chimpanzees, as well as a number of lesser-known but highly threatened creatures, including the white-breasted guinea fowl, white-necked rock fowl, pygmy hippopotamus, Jentink's duiker (a small forest antelope) and the Liberian mongoose. In 1983, nearly 500 square miles of the country's most spectacular rain forest was

171

WHITE-NECKED ROCK FOWL, GHANA, 2022
PHOTO COURTESY OF OLIVIER LANGRAND

designated to become Sapo National Park—Liberia's equivalent of Yellowstone—but the civil unrest that erupted in 1989 brought wildlife conservation efforts to an abrupt halt.

Rescued from the rebel forces of warlord Charles Taylor (who would later be convicted of crimes against humanity), Alex and his family sought refuge in Southern California, where they spent several years before it was safe to return to Liberia. In the fall of 1994, he asked me to accompany him and Karl Kranz, one of my colleagues at the Philadelphia Zoo. I had been hired to develop the Zoo's wildlife conservation program, while Karl managed the animal collection. In his younger days, Karl spent time in Liberia as a Peace Corps volunteer. The three of us hoped to visit the proposed Sapo National Park and resurrect the SCNL, which had disbanded temporarily due to the national conflict.

The day prior to our arrival in Liberia, rebel forces lobbed a number of mortar shells into the capital city of Monrovia. Alex, Karl and I took up residence at what was considered a safe hotel

CARACAL, ENTEBBE ZOO, UGANDA, 2019

BLUE DUIKER, ABIDJAN ZOO, CÔTE D'IVOIRE, 1994

downtown, along with other foreigners who hoped to help Liberian officials restore some semblance of order. Nigerian peace-keeping forces protected the streets of the capital under United Nations' authority. A number of refugee camps were scattered throughout Monrovia, filled with people who had fled the countryside for safety. They had the legitimate fear of torture or death at the bloodied hands of roaming gangs of heavily-armed rebels, many of them in their teens and high on drugs.

CHILDREN AT THE NEW MINISTRY OF HEALTH DISPLACEMENT CAMP
MONROVIA, LIBERIA, 1994

Travel outside Monrovia was ill-advised. We visited a number of government ministers hoping to arrange transport to Sapo by helicopter. The UN had but two helicopters in the country, and only one might be available to us. The other was in the shop awaiting repair. Artillery fire hit it during its last mission. Grounded, we decided to visit what was left of the abandoned Monrovia Zoo and Animal Orphanage. Tragically, whatever animals had been there when the fighting began were now long gone. Rebel forces and starving city residents killed and ate the eagles, snakes, duikers, chimps, leopards and more. We walked into what had been the forest elephant exhibit, home to an orphaned young animal whose mother had been killed years earlier for her ivory and meat. Wildlife officials rescued the youngster and brought it to safety at the Zoo. Unfortunately, the tiny pachyderm would meet the same fate as its mother. It was killed and butchered where it fell. The only remnants of its existence were a few small rib bones strewn about the overgrown grass. I looked down and noticed a couple of spent rifle cartridges, grisly reminders of war's impact on wildlife that now sit on my office shelf.

Later that week, Alex, Karl and I met Johnny Clarke, an old man who had fled his village two years earlier and hid from rebels in the jungle. He told of seeing the rare pygmy hippopotamus on occasion, but not being physically able to kill one for food. He watched from the forest as chimpanzees and other creatures scavenged crops on abandoned farms. The very next day, we met a young woman by the name of Lula Bestman. Lula told us that she was searching for her father who had disappeared two years earlier. A coincidence perhaps? Not at all. As it turned out, Lula was Johnny's married daughter. And, less than 24 hours later, we were able to reunite the family, bringing tears to the eyes of all involved.

Our success on that front, however, was not matched in our attempts to travel in Liberia. Despite all our efforts, the authorities would not allow us to travel outside Monrovia. Biding our time and hoping things might change, we visited a number of sites within the city limits. At the University of Liberia, we observed students taking final exams, standing outside the classrooms and peering through pizza-sized holes in walls that had been peppered by rebel mortar fire. That afternoon, Alex led us along a forest trail to a mass grave where thousands of innocent civilians had been massacred and buried.

SAPO POSTER
ARTWORK COURTESY OF LUCI BETTI NASH

In countryside villages, we observed local people paying homage to the "forest devil," a powerful spirit that is both feared and revered. Walking the streets of Monrovia, we encountered shop owners hawking the skins of various felines: leopards, caracals, servals and golden cats. Others sold bushmeat—mostly duikers. Many of these animals were freshly killed, but some were still alive and would only be dispatched after being purchased. The day ended with a visit to a refugee camp where hundreds of displaced families sought safety from the surrounding conflict, hoping that one day they would be able to return to their homes.

Ultimately, our team was unable to visit Sapo, but that didn't dampen our enthusiasm for establishing Liberia's first national park. Upon our return to the States, we continued to raise funds to resurrect the Society for the Conservation of Nature of Liberia, allowing Alex to hire staff. We commissioned my good friend and artist Luci Betti Nash to create a poster that promoted the creation of Sapo National Park. We also launched a relief campaign for the poor souls still living in refugee camps,

filling cargo containers with clothes and much-needed supplies. All of this fell under the umbrella of our Adopt Sapo campaign. Official documents list 1983 as the year Sapo National Park was created, but it wasn't until after the civil war ended in 1996 that the designation truly took hold.

In 2000, Alex received the prestigious Goldman Environmental Prize for his efforts to protect and preserve Liberia's natural heritage. As further testament to his life's work, the country now boasts three national parks, two more having been established since Sapo: Gola National Park on the western border with Sierra Leone and Grebo-Krahn National Park on the eastern border with Côte d'Ivoire.

A few weeks ago, I was ferreting through my Liberia project files and came across a newspaper, *First National Poll*, that I'd saved from my 1994 visit. The headline: "2000 Women, Children Massacred." The report detailed a slaughter in the town of Gbarnga, about 100 miles from where I had been staying in Monrovia. I recall reading the article the day it hit the newsstands by candlelight in my hotel room, and deciding that it probably would be best if my wife didn't see it, at least not right away. So, when I returned home, I tucked it away in a filing cabinet and forgot about it. Fast forward a quarter century, and here I was

Liberia lies

at the center of the Guinean Forests of West Africa, a global hotspot of biological diversity. It encompasses the largest tracts of forests remaining in the region. Despite that, the survival of close to one thousand species within the hotspot remains under threat including the forest elephant and pygmy hippopotamus. Among the primates, red colobus monkey and chimpanzee populations are the most seriously affected. Habitat loss and hunting continue to pose a serious threat.

PYGMY HIPPOPOTAMUS, ABIDJAN ZOO, CÔTE D'IVOIRE, 1994

rummaging through my Liberia files. I felt that enough time had passed and decided to share it with Nan. I handed it to her and then instinctively took a step back. Her eyebrows shot upwards as she read the headline, then her lips pursed and frown lines crossed her forehead. "And now you know why I worry when you travel to places where nobody in their right mind would ever want to go."

LESSON LEARNED:

Sometimes it's best to hold back a few details when telling a story, for the listener's sake.

AFRICAN FOREST ELEPHANT, GABON, 2006

BROWN BEAR, ALASKA WILDLIFE CONSERVATION CENTER, 2005

HEY, BEAR!

The other day, I met a bear,
A great big bear, Oh way out there.
He looked at me, I looked at him,
He sized up me, I sized up him.
He said to me, "Why don't you run?
I see you ain't, Got any gun."
I said to him, "That's a good idea."
"Now legs get going, get me out of here!

"I Met a Bear" (Traditional American Camp Song)

Each time the grizzly lowered its head to feed, we moved a step or two closer. I was with Haroldo Castro and John Martin, colleagues from Conservation International, and we were at least 50 miles deep into Alaska's Denali National Park. Nothing but knee-high shrubs and wildflowers stood between us and the huge bruin. We had approached close enough that his face could almost fill the zoom lens on Haroldo's video camera—pretty scary when you're staring at a creature that can weigh a quarter-ton or more. Add to that a set of claws as effective as Swiss Army knives and a bite force easily capable of snapping a two-by-four in half or crushing a human bone like a twig. The grizzly, or brown bear of North America, is an animal that deserves our respect, and that's exactly what we gave this one as we inched closer toward him.

The bear turned his head for a glance in our direction. Satisfied that we posed no threat, he resumed munching on his late afternoon meal of blueberries and soapberries. Winter was

WILLOW PTARMIGAN, GLACIER NATIONAL PARK, MONTANA, 2004

approaching and the bear's need for calories was pressing, so eating was a clear priority. The three puny humans that had entered his territory were worth watching, but not a significant distraction or worth the energy of chasing, even though any one of us would have provided substantially more nutrition than a meal of berries. *Should* the bear have decided to attack, well, that would've ended our trip.

Haroldo, John and I were in Alaska shooting a promotional video for our upcoming book, *Wilderness: Earth's Last Wild Places*. Roughly equivalent in size to the state of Massachusetts, Denali National Park has both boreal forest and arctic tundra. Together, these two ecosystems encircle the top of the globe and cover close to a quarter of Earth's land surface. The forests

are simple in structure: a single-layered canopy, a sparse shrub layer and a ground cover of lichens and mosses. Winters last half the year and precipitation is low. The same is true of the barren tundra, essentially a frozen desert where no self-respecting tree would expect to grow. Both regions are largely uninhabited by humans, but the native fauna is nothing short of spectacular: moose, elk, caribou, mountain sheep and goats, brown, black and polar bears, timber wolves, musk oxen, walrus, bald eagles, ptarmigan and more.

ELK, ALASKA WILDLIFE CONSERVATION CENTER, 2005

Those who know grizzlies well—people who live or regularly work in bear country—agree on a number of things that people should do to avoid an attack. Experts suggest that you make your presence known to the bear from the get-go by doing such things as jingling a set of "bear bells" and repeating the words "Hey, bear" as you hike. No bear startled, lower risk of an attack. That being said, I've read accounts of people who apparently did everything by the book, but still ended up mauled. They hit the ground and played dead, but that didn't prevent or halt the grizzly's attack. The bears, you see, don't read safety instructions or survival manuals.

It's especially dangerous to come between a sow (female bear) and her cubs. I made that mistake once, or I should say that the bear cub made the mistake of getting between its mom and me. I had little choice in the matter. It wasn't a grizzly, but rather a black bear and her cubs in Yellowstone National Park. My Uncle Jim and I were walking up the trail to Tower Falls when this young black bear ambled across our path, just beyond its mother's gaze. Rosie, its mom, was well-known to park rangers. She and her progeny across several seasons had earned quite a reputation for interacting with visitors, to the point that Rosie became a nuisance and, at times, dangerous. Several times she was captured and transported to remote regions of the Park, only to eventually get her bearings (no pun intended) and

Wilderness:

Earth's Last Wild Places details a study that spotlights the terrestrial regions of our planet that remain largely undisturbed, sparsely populated by humans and replete with native wildlife. At the turn of the present century, we discovered that nearly half of Earth's land area—deserts, savannas, wetlands, woodlands, tundra, and tropical, montane and boreal forests—is still pristine. Our findings give hope to conservationists who are focused on safeguarding wilderness plants and animals.

BROWN BEAR, DENALI NATIONAL PARK, ALASKA, 2002
PHOTO COURTESY OF JOHN MARTIN

return to her former haunts. My run-in with one of Rosie's cubs (I believe it was either Yogi or Boo Boo, seriously) falls comfortably in the "no harm, no foul" category. The little guy stood still only long enough for me to snap a quick photo, then went on his merry way down the trail and back into the woods behind me. All I ever saw of Mom was a silhouette against a line of backlit tree trunks a bit farther up the slope.

Bear experts universally agree on another thing when it comes to encounters: The absolute *worst thing* you can do is turn tail and run from an attacking bear. Bears are predators, hardwired to chase down prey. Even a portly adult grizzly can hit 30 miles per hour in the snap of a finger—faster than any Olympic sprinter who has ever lived.

As Haroldo, John and I watched our grizzly munching berries, I recalled a somewhat similar experience I once had with an alligator near the Florida Everglades. I was with my sister Donna in the Loxahatchee National Wildlife Refuge. The gator was basking open-mouthed in a shallow pool carpeted with water hyacinths. While Donna stayed back at a picnic table, I approached the animal slowly, one step at a time, wanting to take a position close enough for a profile photo. An older gentleman and his wife watched me from the picnic bench near my sister. I heard them talking as I inched toward the alligator. The husband wanted to take a close-up as well. "Look at that, honey. Look how close he's getting to the alligator. And it doesn't even seem to notice him."

The man's wife wasn't impressed. Nor did she approve of my behavior. "Don't even *think* about going down there. Alligators attack people all the time. That fool is taking a big risk." At that point, I stopped and looked back at the couple, smiling and waving to let them know I could hear everything they were saying. I imagine that pissed off the woman even more, so I returned to my task of getting a photo. Moving three or four feet closer to the large reptile, I stopped, knelt, snapped the shutter, took another few measured steps, stopped, knelt, took another photo, and found myself just a tad more than two gator's lengths away from my subject.

This is how I approach most wild creatures that

An alligator

or a crocodile lying still with its mouth wide open is most likely not a threat. The animal may simply be regulating its body temperature by allowing heat to escape from the moist surfaces of its tongue, teeth and palate. Unable to sweat as humans do or pant like dogs, these ancient reptiles rely on a more passive means of cooling, which the average person might misread as a warning.

AMERICAN ALLIGATOR AT LOXAHATCHEE NATIONAL WILDLIFE REFUGE, FLORIDA, 1999

I'm photographing: one or two steps at a time, doing my best not to spook or disturb them. It's a technique that works just as well with a rabbit as a bird or even a rhino. It's important to consider what the animal is doing, why it's doing it, and what its comfort level might be concerning your approach. To be sure, it greatly helps to be an animal behaviorist so that you don't misread their signs.

Finally, the husband couldn't stand it anymore. He got up from the picnic bench and declared, "I'm going to get my alligator picture!"

He'd taken only a few strides when his wife jumped off the bench and yelled, "Alligators can run 25 miles an hour! *You can't*!" He'd

ALASKA RANGE NEAR DENALI NATIONAL PARK, 2002

heard her but didn't break stride, so she chastised me as well. "Young man, alligators can run 25 miles an hour. If you can't run that fast, you'd better get out of there!"

The setup couldn't have been more perfect. Drum roll, please! "Ma'am, I don't need to run 25 miles an hour!" Cue the cymbal! "I just need to run *faster* than your husband!"

If anything could be better than perfect, this was it. She was the Gracie to my George Burns. The two of us could have taken the show on the road.

The big bruin paused from his endless feast and looked up which snapped my attention back to the task at hand in Denali. Haroldo, John and I watched Mr. Grizzly as though through the eyes of a hawk. We hadn't discussed an escape strategy should the grizzly feel threatened, but I gave the situation some serious thought. Had the bear stopped eating, turned in our direction,

or begun to stare, I would stand still, encourage my colleagues to do likewise, and keep my eyes fixed on the bear. In essence, he would be telling us "Okay fellas, that's a wrap." Even if he had resumed eating immediately afterward, my advice would be to back off, content with whatever video Haroldo had shot. Were the bear to charge, I planned to go primeval—scream at the top of my lungs and hurl my camera in his face—hoping that either Haroldo or John would finish telling this story.

Fortunately, no such action was necessary. The next time the three of us saw our bear it was larger than life on the big screen at the National Geographic Society, the night our *Wilderness* book launched. The auditorium was at capacity. Nan and both my parents were there and they even stood in line after the presentation to have their books signed. It was one of the most rewarding moments of my life.

LESSON LEARNED:

Always be observant around wild creatures. Consider the advice of biologists who regularly observe or interact with them, and never let your guard down. Animal behavior is predictable. Usually.

GOLDEN FROG, PANAMA'S EL VALLE AMPHIBIAN CONSERVATION CENTER, 2008
PUBLISHED IN *NATIONAL GEOGRAPHIC KIDS*, 2008

THE INCREDIBLE
FROG HOTEL

The fly said to the frog, "Time flies when you're having fun."
The frog replied, "Actually, time's fun when you're having flies!"

Unknown Origin

"**Y**ou're a real frog wrangler, aren't you?"

The studio audience chuckled at my question. Standing beside me on stage, Martha Stewart was deftly catching a couple of maverick amphibians that were hopping about on the table. She gently captured each one and returned it to its mossy mini-habitat. The fat, orangey-red, aptly-named tomato frog from Madagascar had wobbled off to her left. Just to be contrary, the lanky golden frog from Panama was making tracks to the right, employing a somewhat herky-jerky, keep-on-truckin' mode of locomotion. This segment of the celebrity chef's show was not a demonstration of the best frog leg recipes. Martha was highlighting an international effort to save the world's vanishing frogs, toads and salamanders from a deadly global pandemic.

As she wrangled a handful of frogs, a runaway fungus called *chytrid* was decimating wild amphibian populations across continents. Several species had already gone extinct, while others, including the exquisite Panamanian golden frog, had disappeared from the wild and were barely hanging on in several bio-secure facilities.

The golden frog, as its name might suggest, is a jewel-like creature and a prominent national symbol in its native Panama. Its image appears on currency, stamps, clothing, jewelry, paintings, signage and an almost endless variety of curios that are snatched up by tourists in quaint shops and outdoor village markets. Among my very favorite knickknacks are little painted clay figurines—golden frogs smooching one another across a heart-shaped lily pad or ordering drinks at a bar—none of which seem the least bit concerned about the impending fungal invasion.

The prognosis

for wild amphibian populations exposed to the chytrid fungus is not promising. The pathogen is unlikely to disappear from areas it has invaded, the number of chytrid-free regions is small, and only about one in 10 affected populations show signs of recovery after exposure. As far as scientists know, less than two percent of the world's more than 6,000 amphibian species have disappeared due to chytrid but, of course, extinction is forever.

The origins of the chytrid fungus continue to be debated, but the effects of the disease it causes in amphibians are gruesomely obvious. It attacks and hardens layers of a frog's skin that contain keratin, the same substance found in our fingernails and hair or the horn of a rhinoceros. Chytrid also damages the amphibian nervous system. Frogs not only breathe through their lungs but also their skin, so when the fungus hardens keratin, it effectively suffocates them. The skin becomes discolored and peels off. Infected frogs are sluggish and sit unprotected in the open, unlike healthy animals that would take cover from danger. Infected frogs lose their appetites and stop eating. Their bodies become rigid. Death is certain. The first chytrid cases came to light in Australia in the early 1990s, but no efforts to date have been able to halt the fungus' global spread, which has reached at least 60 countries.

HERPETOLOGIST EDGARDO GRIFFITH SEARCHES FOR GOLDEN FROGS, PANAMA, 2006

In May 2006, I found myself wading through a shallow mountain stream in the hills overlooking the sleepy town of El Valle de Anton. Leading the way was Panamanian herpetologist Edgardo Griffith, an expert on his country's native reptiles and amphibians. In the crystal clear water, we easily spotted the brightly-colored frogs. Edgardo explained that the males were waiting patiently for the females to arrive so that they might get down to the business of mating. The ladies were traveling overland. They would have to climb down the vegetation to enter the water and meet their mates. Sure enough, Edgardo pointed up ahead on the left bank where one was descending to the stream.

For months, Edgardo, Heidi Ross (his soon-to-be wife) and a handful of American colleagues had been busy collecting golden frogs and many other amphibians from the Rio Maria and nearby sites to stock a captive breeding program. It was in every sense a

PANAMANIAN GOLDEN FROG, LOS ALTOS DEL MARIA, PANAMA, 2006

last-ditch effort to save these species from extinction. Our brief afternoon stream survey suggested that the fungus had yet to arrive in these particular hills, but Edgardo and his colleagues knew it was only a matter of time. El Valle's golden frogs—one of the last surviving wild populations—were at serious risk of being wiped out. In fact, one year later, no one could find a trace of this species in the wild. The only thing standing between it (and other Panamanian species) and the tragedy of the ill-fated dodo were the animals taken into captivity to establish an insurance colony.

It was indeed fortunate that Edgardo, Heidi and their international team of volunteers had not been caught napping. At the time that they launched the rescue mission, no special facility existed in Panama for housing these amphibian refugees. Quick thinking was imperative. The duo played a long shot and asked the proprietor of the nearby Hotel Campestre if they

THE HOTEL CAMPESTRE, EL VALLE DE ANTON, PANAMA, 2006

could book a few rooms—not for themselves but for some frogs, toads and salamanders. Without hesitation, the hotel agreed to provide rooms for the project for as long as necessary.

Martha Stewart's producer read about this "Incredible Frog Hotel" while thumbing through *National Geographic Kids* magazine. What was first meant to be a quarter-page column had blossomed into a four-page spread, stacked with a rainbow array of amphibians: glistening frogs the color of ripe lemons and tangerines, coffee-colored tree frogs, emerald green leaf frogs, azure blue poison dart frogs, robber frogs that looked as if they'd been sculpted from vanilla ice cream, and horned frogs that appeared dipped in tanning lotion.

Although amphibian accommodations at the Hotel Campestre weren't ideal, they were more than adequate for the job at hand. An international team of herpetologists worked 24-7 to maintain

GHOST FROG, EVACC, PANAMA, 2008

the growing animal collection. Project Golden Frog's rescue mission took up three rooms. Anyone walking into a room had to first step into a mild disinfecting bath of chlorine beach. This killed any fungus that might try to sneak in on the soles of someone's shoes or sandals. Likewise, any plant material or hardware that made its way into the rooms had to be disinfected. One or two folks worked outside on the veranda, spraying and dousing the plastic containers before handing them through the doorway. Inside, Heidi busily changed out the temporary plastic containers that were provided for the dozens of fragile creatures under her care. The routine consumed hours and is easily the most dedicated combination of room service and intensive care that I have ever witnessed.

As the new director of conservation at the Houston Zoo, part of my job was to ensure the continuation of these emergency measures and oversee the construction of the biosecure El Valle Amphibian Conservation Center (EVACC). Working

BLUE PHASE OF THE GREEN-AND-BLACK POISON DART FROG, PANAMA, 2008
PUBLISHED IN *NATIONAL GEOGRAPHIC KIDS*, 2008

ROSIE, ROSENBERG'S TREE FROG, EVACC, PANAMA, 2008

197

VOLUNTEER DISINFECTS PLANTS, THE HOTEL CAMPESTRE, PANAMA, 2007

with private landowners, my colleagues in Houston had found a suitable site on the grounds of the small, privately-owned El Nispero Zoo, located just across the valley from the Hotel Campestre.

TRANSFER OF AMPHIBIANS FROM THE HOTEL CAMPESTRE TO EVACC, PANAMA, 2007

Teams from the Houston Zoo's Facilities and Maintenance Department flew down periodically to help local laborers construct EVACC. Two-thirds of the building would serve as a breeding facility and scientific laboratory, sufficient to house small populations of the most threatened species. The remaining third of the building would welcome Panamanians and tourists who could observe native amphibians in naturalistic exhibits.

For the frogs, toads and salamanders, checkout at the hotel came on the morning of March 14, 2007. Our international team stacked amphibian-filled plastic containers one atop the other and loaded them into waiting vehicles. It was a handsome procession, but no fanfare or fireworks, just our own private little frog parade slowly making its way through the town. One of the vehicles escorted Rosie, for now, the sole representative of the rare Rosenberg's gladiator frog. Also along for the ride

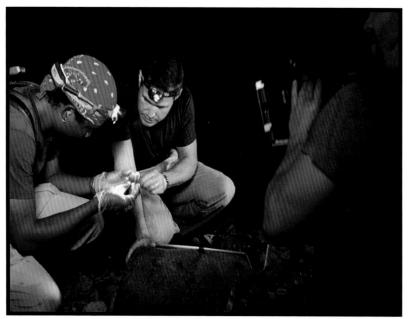

ANIMAL PLANET PRODUCTION OF *THE VANISHING FROG*, PANAMA, 2008

was a species unknown to science at the time. We had a few of these frogs that were eventually described as a new species, but in the end, they did not survive.

About a year later, I received a telephone call from Jeff Corwin of Animal Planet. Jeff had heard about EVACC and felt our story would make an important addition to *The Vanishing Frog*, a documentary he was making. He and his film crew planned to highlight three or four amphibian conservation projects in the Americas, drawing attention to the global impacts of chytrid. If the fungus could be brought under control in the wild or if it could be shown that the disease sometimes moves through a region but eventually dissipates, then perhaps one day animals safeguarded in captivity could be returned to their natural habitats on an experimental basis. Not out of the realm of possibility was the hope that some wild populations might weather the storm and be able to repopulate their tropical forest homes after the pandemic had run its course.

ROBBER FROG, EVACC, PANAMA, 2008
PUBLISHED IN *NATIONAL GEOGRAPHIC KIDS,* 2008

The documentary, *A Leap of Faith*, chronicled the effort to save the Panamanian golden frog. My good friend and colleague, wildlife videographer Dan Breton, produced it. The English version played for years in American zoos that exhibit and breed this species, while a Spanish version, *Un Salta de Fe*, was used as an educational tool at EVACC and in Panamanian schools.

A few years ago, I picked up a copy of *The Sixth Extinction: An Unnatural History* by Elizabeth Kolbert. In it, she describes five global extinction events over the past 500 million years, each of which essentially ravaged Earth's resident biological diversity at the time. Kolbert contends that we may very well be on the path to a sixth such catastrophic event. In chapter one, the first sentence reads, "The town of El Valle de Anton, in central Panama, sits in the middle of a volcanic crater formed about a million years ago." At the bottom of the next page, following some background on the impacts of the chytrid epidemic,

HEIDI CHECKS OUT THE NEW ACCOMMODATIONS, EVACC, PANAMA, 2007

Kolbert states, "I first read about the frogs of El Valle in a nature magazine for children that I picked up from my kids. The article, which was illustrated with full-color photos of the Panamanian golden frog, and other brilliantly colored species, told the story of the spreading scourge and the biologists' efforts to get out in front of it." I found it incredibly rewarding to learn that efforts to save a tiny frog in the jungles of Central America had inspired a Pulitzer Prize-winning book that would help galvanize the international conservation community.

Although biologists continue to search and survey Central American forests for amphibians that have vanished to the human eye, they have not found any wild populations of Panamanian golden frogs for more than a decade. The species is still considered to be extinct in the wild.

Meanwhile, a study led by scientists at the Australian National University has documented the extinction of more than 90 amphibian species worldwide in the past 50 years; eight of those species were native to Panama. EVACC's success helped spawn the Panama Amphibian Rescue Conservation Project, a collaboration between the Smithsonian Institution and a number of North American zoological parks and aquariums, as well as similar efforts throughout Central and South America. The hope is to breed animals with an inherited resistance to chytrid so that wild populations can be re-established in areas where they have disappeared.

LESSON LEARNED:
A threatened species should only be considered "saved" when it continues to exist in the wild—not just in zoos, aquariums, laboratories or special breeding centers. The job is incomplete until its survival in nature is assured.

IN SEARCH OF THE
KOOLOO-KAMBA

A gorilla walks into a bar and orders a martini.
The bartender doesn't believe it at first, but mixes the drink and
hands it to the gorilla, who hands him a twenty-dollar bill in return.
The bartender puts the twenty in the cash register
and gives the gorilla a five-dollar bill in change.
"You know," the bartender says,
"we don't get too many gorillas in here."
The gorilla replies, "At fifteen bucks a drink, I'm not surprised."

Author's version of an old joke

The best part of working for the Houston Zoo (with apologies to my many Bayou City friends) was not living in Houston. Hired in 2003 to revitalize the Zoo's Naturally Wild conservation program, I worked largely from home in Pennsylvania. I reported to my longtime friend and colleague, zoo director Rick Barongi. Our paths crossed numerous times since our Cornell days in the early 1970s. While I enjoyed stints at several large international conservation organizations, Rick held high-level positions at the Miami Metrozoo, San Diego Zoo and Disney's Animal Kingdom before moving to Houston. During the five years we worked together, he sent me on assignments to Panama, Malaysia, Tanzania, Kenya, Gabon and Rwanda.

In 2006, I headed to the Central African nation of Gabon. First, though, let's turn back the clock by about 150 years for a little background.

April 6, 1865: French explorer Paul Du Chaillu's journal entry tells of a local African hunter's encounter with an ape that Du Chaillu believed was unknown to science. Returning to camp after dark, the hunter, Malaouen, reported that "... he had heard the cry of the kooloo, and knew where to find it in the morning." Du Chaillu also heard the call but didn't know what animal had made it. Based on the hunter's description, the Frenchman deduced it was almost certainly a new species of ape, which the local people called *kooloo-kamba*. *Kooloo* for the sound it made, *kamba* meaning "to speak."

The kooloo was believed to be very rare, so Du Chaillu was not confident about finding one. Still, he and his men awoke early the next day and set out in two separate parties. After about an hour in the forest, he heard the animal's cry, looked up to see the ape in the branches above and fired at it immediately. The animal fell to the ground. Examining it, Du Chaillu believed it was neither a chimpanzee nor a gorilla, but a species somewhere in between and new to science. No evidence of the creature, other than Du Chaillu's journal entry, remains.

In July 2006, the Houston Zoo launched a fact-finding expedition to Gabon to collect information that would help design a new African rain forest exhibit, and I was invited to go. Our in-country travel would take us through Du Chaillu's kooloo-kamba territory. We weren't focused on establishing the legend's validity, but our journey provided an opportunity to gather local knowledge of the purported primate.

Early in our trek, we visited an ape rescue mission on the shores of Lake Evaro, not very far downriver from the late humanitarian Dr. Albert Schweitzer's tropical field hospital at Lambaréné. At Evaro, we met a young African animal caretaker named Jean. Among his charges were several orphaned apes, including three young gorillas and two chimpanzees. Jean's job as a surrogate parent was to hand-raise his little troop of chimpanzees and gorillas so that one day they might be returned to the wild.

RICK AND ME ON THE TRAIL TO IVINDO NATIONAL PARK, GABON, 2006

Before coming to Evaro, Jean had worked at British zoo owner and gambling magnate John Aspinall's gorilla sanctuary in the neighboring country of Congo. Jean and a friend had been speaking to some of the local people when they ran into poachers who resented the intrusion and the threat to their livelihood. The poachers shot both him and his friend. Jean unbuttoned his shirt, pulling back one side to reveal a scar from the bullet wound. His friend, tragically, did not survive.

JEAN THIERRY ELLA BEKE AND HIS CHARGES, GABON, 2006
PHOTO COURTESY OF RAY MENDEZ

My good friend, Ray Mendez, an entomologist, photographer and professional exhibit designer, was a key member of the Houston Zoo team. As the two of us were photographing Jean and his young apes, Ray was visibly impacted by the experience. In his words, "When he walked out of the jungle with a couple of

ORPHANED GORILLA, GABON, 2006

his adopted charges, I was moved to the point of feeling a pain in my chest and I broke out in tears. Nothing I would have expected from a hardened New York City naturalist. Our world is a place of pain if you bother to look at what our species is doing to the planet and our fellow passengers. However, there is hope from the hands of the most unexpected people and places."

A bit farther down the river, similar ape rescue efforts were underway along the shores of the Fernan Vaz Lagoon. In many parts of Africa, poachers routinely kill adult chimpanzees and gorillas for their meat, as well as for their heads, hands and other body parts. They end up as curios and trophies or ingredients in dubious traditional medicines. In almost every case, poachers sell their orphaned infants as pets.

Farther inland, in the forests surrounding Lopé National Park, our team visited the small village of Makoghe. We spent the morning canoeing the river and the afternoon enjoying a dance performance by local children. Their faces painted chalk white and red ochre, the youngsters strode before us, chanting and clapping along with their mothers and aunts who watched proudly from the edge of the clearing. That evening we sat in the eerie glow of a campfire. Into the firelight jumped the

WELCOME DANCE PERFORMED BY VILLAGE CHILDREN, GABON, 2006

village chief, Jean-Jacques Makoukou, who only a short time before swapped his T-shirt and blue jeans for a leopard-spotted bandana, a headdress of parrot feathers, a tooth-filled necklace and a grass loincloth. The transformed chief jumped and gyrated to the primal drumbeat, shaking his white-chalked arms, stomping his feet and chanting words unintelligible to western ears.

Earlier that day, Maude Lafortune, the Houston Zoo's French-speaking veterinarian, interviewed Jean-Jacques about his experiences with the chimpanzees and gorillas of the Lopé region. He told of how, more than 10 years earlier, he had come upon what he described as a chimpanzee that was larger, darker, and longer-armed than any he had ever seen before. He called it *koulanguiki*, as it's known in the local Simba language. The chief said that he had startled the sleeping animal, which fled into the forest. That was the only time Jean-Jacques had ever encountered such a creature, and he knew of no one who had seen it since. Could the animal have been the mythical kooloo-kamba?

FOREST DEVIL DANCE, KAZAMABIKA VILLAGE, GABON, 2007

Myths and legends abound in the Congo forests of Africa, as do long-standing fears of the beasts these jungles are believed to harbor. The notion of "forest devils" persists throughout the region and they turn up regularly in ceremonial dances, such as the one I observed in the village of Kazamabika during a return trip to Gabon in 2007. On that trip, I visited established conservation projects and scouted for more.

This entry from my trip journal describes the incredible performance: "A young man waves palm fronds at the forest edge, coaxing the "devil" from its lair and into a central clearing around which the villagers have gathered. The "spirit being" wears a feathered headdress, a colobus monkey cape, and a mask painted black, white and red. It kicks up clouds of red dust into the air as it pursues its tempter. The villagers chant and sway to the rhythm of drums, both the hand-crafted, hide-covered kind and the 50-gallon steel variety. They coax and cajole the spirit for close to an hour, building confidence and overcoming their fears."

CHRONICLING THE DAY'S EVENTS, MIKONGO CAMP, GABON, 2006
PHOTO COURTESY OF RICK BARONGI

Villagers deal with threats from the forest every day. Crop-raiding elephants can be a real problem. While walking through a village, I came upon a woman tending her cassava patch, which a pachyderm had recently ravaged. All that remained of her crop were stripped and uprooted branches strewn about the trampled soil. Elephants, apparently, relish the cassava's tender leaves and starchy roots. When I arrived, the woman had just finished stringing empty soup and coffee cans around her garden. Small bundles of cans hung from metal wire stretched

FOREST ELEPHANT, GABON, 2006

between the spindly fence posts that she had driven into the ground. The contraption would do little, if anything, to stop any self-respecting elephant, but the clatter and clanging of the cans would alert her to a marauder's presence. The raid would likely occur at night, so she might not hear anything from her home, which wasn't close by. Guarding her garden required that she sleep right there in the field, beneath a makeshift shelter of corrugated tin panels. She had no problem enduring a night in what amounted to a solar oven to confront and do her best to scare off the forest elephant.

Much of Gabon remains covered in pristine tropical rain forests and boasts the world's largest remaining populations of chimpanzees and lowland gorillas. In 2002, Gabon's president Omar Bongo created 13 national parks covering more than 11,500 square miles—fully 10 percent of the country, which is larger than the combined areas of Denali and Yellowstone National Parks in the United States.

The Congo Forests

of Central Africa are the second largest block of tropical rain forest left on Earth and rank among the planet's top four wilderness areas in terms of biological richness. The entire country of Gabon is included within this vast ecoregion. In addition to gorillas, chimpanzees and forest elephants, the rain forest is home to such flagship species as the okapi, red river hog, bongo and goliath frog—the world's largest frog.

I spent many evening hours during our expedition chronicling the events of the day. In addition to the gorillas, chimps and forest elephants, members of our team floated downriver *below* crocodiles basking in trees overhead—you heard that right, crocodiles can and do climb trees. Gabon has 550 miles of shoreline, and it does not disappoint. As our Zodiac boats crashed through breaking waves in the Atlantic Ocean, we caught a glimpse of humpback whales breaching. Gabon is an absolutely magical place and critical to the ecological integrity of Central Africa's Congo Forests.

LESSON LEARNED:

Animal myths and legends survive generations, even centuries, sometimes adding spice to routine biological investigations. Whatever their origins, these tales are best savored for the insights they provide into the realities of the people who call the wilderness their home.

SLENDER SNOUTED CROCODILE, LOANGO NATIONAL PARK, GABON, 2007

BREACHING HUMPBACK WHALE, GABON, 2006

ELOK, OKLAHOMA CITY ZOO, 2017

PONGOS
HELPING
PONGOS

Orangutans teach us that looks are not everything ...

Will Cuppy
How to Tell Your Friends from the Apes (1931)

I own a single piece of what you might call valuable art—an original, abstract painting. Let's just say I paid more for it than any of my other paintings, photos or sculptures. I was at a charity auction, I had enjoyed a few drinks and my wife wasn't around to keep my hand from my wallet. Toss in the fact that proceeds from the Pongos Helping Pongos art auction would help support wildlife conservation in faraway lands, and I was a fish just begging to be hooked.

What really drew me to this particular masterpiece were its creators. I met artist Neva Mikulicz for the first time that evening. I wasn't familiar with her work, but that didn't matter because it was the handiwork of her artistic partner that grabbed my attention: Elok was a young male orangutan at the Houston Zoo. The piece is titled *Elok Made Me Do Abstract Art*, a bold and striking blend of cooperative primate creativity. I gathered from the title that Elok was a Jackson Pollock fan.

I met my first wild orangutan in 2006. The opportunity required a short hike through a swampy, leech-infested patch of forest, but it was well worth the effort. A mother orangutan and her

ELOK MADE ME DO ABSTRACT ART
PAINTING BY NEVA MIKULICZ AND ELOK THE ORANGUTAN IN 2008

clinging infant hung about 80 or so feet above me and my host, Dr. Marc Ancrenaz. They were suspended in true quadrumanous fashion—all four appendages serving as hands. Marc stands at least a head taller than me, so he had a slightly better view of

YOUNG BORNEAN ORANGUTAN, THE SEPILOK ORANGUTAN REHAB CENTER, 2006

the duo. I met Marc and his wife, Isabelle, in the early 1990s, shortly after they created the nonprofit organization Hutan and launched the Kinabatangan Orangutan Conservation Project (KOCP) in Sabah, Malaysian Borneo. My trip to Sabah was courtesy of Charlie Perlitz, a donor to the Houston Zoo who wanted to see the world's great apes—chimpanzees, gorillas and orangutans—in their natural habitats.

Zoo Director Rick Barongi introduced me to Charlie. The two got to know one another on a birding trip to Panama. Charlie later asked Rick to help arrange an excursion to Borneo. Over dinner at a small Houston seafood restaurant, Rick handed Charlie's request to me since primates are my specialty. I suggested that Charlie visit Kinabatangan, a place that I was keen to scope out for conservation possibilities. Charlie agreed and then asked if

OXBOW LAKE ALONG THE KINABATANGAN RIVER, SABAH, MALAYSIA, 2006

I was willing to accompany him. My response was quick and to the point, "Okay, as long as we're clear that I'm treating this as a site visit for a zoo conservation project, a chance to see firsthand what our support is doing to help orangutans in the wild. I'm not going as a tour guide."

Charlie nodded in agreement and thus began the first of three international adventures he and I would share over the next few years. Once we had settled on the Borneo itinerary, Charlie stopped in at the Zoo, dropped off a check for $10,000, and explained, "This should cover Bill's expenses for the trip. Anything left over goes straight into the conservation program."

Pongo is the name of the primate genus that includes the orangutans of both Borneo (one species) and Sumatra (two species). All three species are critically endangered due to not only the continuing loss of their tropical forest habitat but also deadly conflict with humans. Orangutans like to eat a number of plantation-grown fruits such as durian, jackfruit, mangoes, mangosteen and rambutan. They're also very fond of tender young palm shoots. Their tastes put them at odds with farmers who may retaliate by shooting at crop raiders. There's also a never-ending market for young orangutans as pets. The trade is illegal, but that seems to be of little consequence.

The name "orangutan" comes from the Malay words *orang* (person) and *hutan* (forest). Thus, an orangutan is a "person of the forest." Our shaggy, red-haired relatives are the most arboreal of all the great apes, spending the vast majority of their time in the trees. Adult males typically dwarf females and are easily distinguished by their large fleshy cheek pads or flanges, even at a distance. When not in sight, their characteristic long calls give them away. Younger, unflanged males, on the other hand, are not nearly as robust as their more mature and dominant relatives, making it difficult sometimes to tell the boys from the girls, especially at a distance. Both sexes are largely solitary, except when mothers are caring for their young. Fruit is the orangutan's dietary mainstay, supplemented with leaves, bark, honey, insects, and bird's eggs, and can sustain an animal for some 40 to 50 years in the wild.

The Kinabatangan

Wildlife Sanctuary—a 500-kilometer-long mosaic of riparian forests, oxbow lakes, swamps and mangroves—is home to Asian elephants and 10 species of primates: the Bornean orangutan, Bornean gibbon, proboscis monkey, silvered langur, maroon langur, Hose's langur, long-tailed macaque, pig-tailed macaque, slow loris and western tarsier. Carnivores include the clouded leopard, leopard cat, marbled cat and flat-headed cat, as well as the Malay sun bear—the world's smallest bear.

OIL PALM PLANTATIONS AND REFINERY, SABAH, MALAYSIA, 2006

Marc and Isabelle and their team were based in the Kinabatangan Wildlife Sanctuary, named for the river and its floodplain of more than 60,000 acres. Much of the region had been logged well before the couple's arrival, and the land largely became agricultural. Today, oil palm plantations are all too common, yet the area remains a haven for orangutans, nine other primate species, Asian elephants and more than 250 bird species. The forests are particularly flush with hornbills—large-billed birds that resemble modern-day pterodactyls.

On our way from the Kota Kinabalu International Airport to Kinabatangan, Marc, Charlie and I stopped to stock up on a few essentials for the days ahead. No orangutan could fail to be tempted by one of the riches of these markets. Golden-yellow bunches of bananas hung above a giant fruit bowl filled with papaya, pineapple, mango, mangosteen, lychee, rambutan and more. The large, spiky durian, known as "the king of fruits," was also clearly present, if not by sight, certainly by its aroma. Durian is a delicacy for both man and red ape, but, as they say, it is an acquired taste. Its odor has been likened to rotting meat, turpentine and sweaty gym socks, or some combination of the three. Chemists have identified nearly 50 organic compounds that contribute to the skunk-like aroma. You can eat durian raw or use it as a flavoring in cooking, and some maintain it can reduce fevers. Marc bought several of these bad boys and stored them under thick rags as far back in the vehicle as possible.

On our 200-mile drive from Kota Kinabalu to Sukau, we passed endless acres of oil palm plantations and trucks loaded to the brim with bunches of palm nuts. Malaysia is the world's second-largest palm oil producer, trailing only Indonesia in terms of plantation coverage. Every few miles, the smokestack of a palm oil refinery jutted above the treetops.

A day or two after we arrived at the Sanctuary, Marc and I loaded a couple of durian fruits (their stench already beginning to permeate the research camp) and a six-pack of beer into a small boat. We set off on a moonlight adventure. Spotlighting the treetops, we caught the eyeshine of numerous slow lorises, small and prickly primates that hunt insects in the black of night. We also startled sleeping proboscis monkeys—huge balls of fur in tree branches overhanging the water—who bed down together in family groups. The dominant males with their huge fleshy Jimmy Durante noses threatened us as our boat coasted beneath them. Borneo, the world's third-largest island, is the only place you'll find proboscis monkeys in the wild.

Our boat drifted a bit farther. Marc suggested that I close my eyes and smell the air. The sweet scent of lush forest filled my nostrils. Then the aroma abruptly changed, becoming sour and musty with the slightest hint of gasoline. "Now open your eyes and look up," Marc instructed, pointing his flashlight back up into the treetops. I followed the beam to another huddled proboscis group. "You can smell these monkeys before you see them."

CHARLIE PERLITZ AND MARC ANCRENAZ, KINABATANGAN ORANGUTAN CONSERVATION PROJECT, SABAH, MALAYSIA, 2006

Charlie didn't accompany us on our nighttime cruise, nor did he come along for the short hike through the leech-laden marsh to see orangutans. I quickly learned that he was not the hiking type but quite efficient at expending the minimal amount of energy to achieve his goals. He decided that the best place for him to see orangutans "in the wild" was at the Sepilok Nature Reserve in the city of Sandakan. So, Charlie chartered a small private boat that took him 60 miles upriver, where he promised to meet Marc and me in a couple of days. At exactly one o'clock in the afternoon, Marc and I should expect to find him in the Sepilok parking lot. I took his promise of punctuality with the proverbial grain of salt.

As I mentioned in an earlier story, Sepilok opened in the early 1960s as a center for orphaned young orangutans rescued from the pet trade. At best, the animals in residence are "semi-wild" or "soon-to-be-wild," since their care is geared toward independence and an eventual return to the surrounding forest.

At exactly one o'clock on the day that we'd arranged, Marc and I stood in the Sepilok parking lot and watched as a taxi pulled up. Charlie emerged from the back seat, paid the driver and walked over to greet us with a big smile on his slightly sunburned face. "Now, gentlemen, let's go see some orangutans!"

Along the path that led to the orangutan feeding station, Marc pointed out a green snake in the vegetation, a deadly viper almost within arm's reach. Clearly, the young orangutans were being given an opportunity to experience some of the dangers faced by their wild relatives. Their communal feeding station consisted of wooden platforms linked by thick ropes that served as vines. There, the youngsters and sub-adults compete for their daily rations of fruits, vegetables and sugar cane with troops of voracious, streetwise macaque monkeys that could never be accused of passing up a free buffet.

It typically requires several years before an individual orangutan develops the necessary climbing, foraging, and social skills to sever ties with its keepers and return to a life in the wild. Some never make that transition and will spend the rest of their lives under human care. I turned to my companions and said, "You know, it was a photo of Russ Mittermeier holding a young orphaned orangutan some 30 or more years ago, right here at this sanctuary, which piqued my interest in primate conservation and set me on the path to where I am today."

When I returned to Houston after the Sabah trip, the primate keepers and curators pulled me aside to share their plans about a program they were launching called Pongos Helping Pongos. It began as an enrichment effort to help the resident orangutans express their intelligence, creative abilities and personalities through painting. Just as importantly, it helped pave the way for zoo orangutans to serve as ambassadors for their threatened wild cousins. The primate staff saw an opportunity to steer the program toward the safeguarding of wild orangutan populations.

ELOK, OKLAHOMA CITY ZOO, 2020
PHOTO COURTESY OF ANDREA JOHNSON

Keepers kept their charges well supplied with brushes, paints, and canvases, and the orangutans kept churning out the artwork. With a truckload of colorful sketches in hand, zoo staff pitched the idea of a charity auction to a local art gallery. The gallery jumped at the opportunity, and Pongos Helping Pongos became an annual event. Over the years, the artwork of the Houston Zoo orangutans has raised tens of thousands of dollars in support of initiatives such as the Kinabatangan Orangutan Conservation Project, and the program's success led to similar creative endeavors by the gibbons and elephants.

The 2008 auction was the first—and I believe the only one—to feature artwork created by both human and animal artists. Elok and Neva's painting was one of five on the auction block.

Elok was born at the Memphis Zoo. His mother had difficulties raising him, so he was transferred to Houston and adopted by an adult female named Cheyenne (after her birthplace, Colorado's

Cheyenne Mountain Zoo). A hybrid, the product of a mating between Bornean and Sumatran parents, Cheyenne will likely never be allowed to breed but is occasionally called upon to foster orphans. Elok was Cheyenne's second foster child, eventually followed by two more.

Not long after the 2008 auction, Elok was sent to the Oklahoma City Zoo on breeding loan. His keepers there describe him as remarkably intelligent, a lover of puzzles, a fan of occasionally playing enrichment games on his iPad and forever interested in taking things apart. Like all orangutans, Elok is incredibly strong and has no problem loosening wrench-tightened nuts and bolts with his bare hands. In Oklahoma, he continues to hone his artistic skills. On International Orangutan Day 2022, artwork created by the 21-year-old, red-haired Picasso became the focus of much attention at a worldwide auction. According to zoo officials, Elok's artwork broke into the digital realm, inspiring the design of a non-fungible token, sales of which benefited his wild cousins as his art has in the past.

LESSON LEARNED:
Animals in captivity can contribute significantly to the survival of their wild relatives. Individual stories and talents provide a treasure chest of highly effective tools for the innovative wildlife conservationist's toolbox.

IGISHA, A SILVERBACK GORILLA, VOLCANOES NATIONAL PARK, RWANDA, 2008

THAT FLIPPIN' GORILLA

Unbelievably, a goldfish can kill a gorilla.
However, it does require a substantial element of surprise ...

George Carlin
When Will Jesus Bring the Pork Chops? (2004)

It suddenly got dark. The sun still blazed brightly overhead, but the shadow of a 400-pound ape loomed over me, eclipsing the daylight. I was kneeling, hunched over on a jungle trail about two-thirds up the slopes of Rwanda's Mount Karisimbi, and there was no escape. A huge black hand reached out and seized the shirt sleeve above my right elbow.

Seven other tourists and I had just hiked for three hours up the southern slope of a dormant volcano, specifically for the opportunity to spend an hour in the backyard of the world's largest primate. The mountain gorilla is also one of our rarest wild relatives—fewer than a thousand have survived decades of encroaching human settlements and civil unrest in this high-altitude, war-torn region of Africa. Mount Karisimbi's peak reaches close to 15,000 feet into the clouds on the international border of Rwanda and the Democratic Republic of Congo. Our trek began at a base camp that sat at 7,000 feet. Following trails used by the gorillas, forest buffalo, and elephants, we climbed to 10,000 feet with the hopes of seeing the more than 40 gorillas known as the Susa Group, named by the late Dian Fossey after the Susa River that runs through its range.

Thick black fingers tightened their grip on my shirt sleeve (of note, this did not include the flesh of my arm). I felt no pinch

VIRUNGA VOLCANOES, RWANDA-DEMOCRATIC REPUBLIC OF CONGO BORDER, 2008

or pressure, but tightened my neck, preparing for the bite I feared could be coming. Only a few minutes before, I had been photographing this impressive creature from what I was told was a safe distance. His name was Igisha, one of four silverback males in the Susa Group.

Prior to embarking, our group of eight was given a very thorough description of what to expect from the gorillas and how to behave to ensure that we all returned safely from our adventure. The rules were simple: first and foremost, be as quiet as possible and stay at least 25 feet from these gentle giants. The Susa Group was one of more than a dozen groups that were well-studied and habituated to tourists. They were tolerant of people observing them at a reasonably close range. Those of us taking photos, and that was everyone, were instructed not to use flashes, which might startle the animals. Most importantly, we should never attempt to touch a gorilla. Physical contact of any kind between visiting humans and the resident apes is strictly verboten, both for safety and health reasons.

Our group ranged in age from the late thirties to the early sixties. Each of us trained to some degree in preparation for the journey. A young Australian woman had just completed an ultra-marathon, so this trek didn't even count as a workout for her.

TREKKING COLLEAGUES IN SEARCH OF THE SUSA GROUP, RWANDA, 2008

The equatorial sun beat down on us as we made our way up the mountain, canceling any cooling effect from the gain in altitude. Swills of bottled water and periodic rest stops defined our ascent. The Susa Group had spent the night a few thousand feet above us and was now moving upwards and feeding as we climbed after them. Unlike the gorillas, we didn't stop to eat, hoping that we could overtake them. Bamboo, wild celery, thistles and nettles—standard gorilla fare—lined our trail. These tough plant fibers slide easily down a gorilla's throat after being rendered a soggy pulp by the animal's large and powerful molars. We humans, on the other hand, don long pants and long-sleeved shirts to protect our arms and legs against the thistle's piercing thorns and the nettle's stinging hairs.

About three hours into our hike, our guide motioned for us to stop. Just ahead, the Susa Group was enjoying an afternoon snack. Large, black, hairy bodies moved about slowly, the occasional arm reaching out to pluck a fistful of greenery. Infants piggybacked on their mothers while youngsters

A FORAGING SILVERBACK PAYING NO ATTENTION TO TOURISTS, RWANDA, 2008

ventured just a bit farther from the family, slowly gaining independence. All was quiet, save for a background of chewing sounds, the occasional belch and the soft brush of vegetation yielding to moving animals. We stopped and waited.

Our team of tourists met the Susa Group at a time when four silverback gorillas—an unusually high number—were contending for the top spot in the dominance hierarchy. The most stable gorilla family groups have a single leader, but two powerful adult males will often vie for the position. More competition for the top position and things can sometimes get a bit dicey. When I "met" the silverback who introduced himself by grabbing me, Igisha was fourth in line and apparently not at all satisfied with his standing. Our guide told us that Igisha occasionally challenged his rivals, but I don't recall him ever mentioning that this particular gorilla occasionally took out his frustrations on tourists as well. That little tidbit, I seem to remember, was something I learned after the fact.

YOUNG MOUNTAIN GORILLA OBSERVING TOURISTS FROM ABOVE, RWANDA, 2008

So, how exactly did I find myself in the grasp of this cantankerous ape? I obeyed all the rules. If I hadn't, our guide would have scolded me, and maybe the guard holding the rifle would have emphasized the point. Armed guards accompany visitors who climb the mountain, hired not only to protect tourists from possible attack by resident forest elephants and buffalo, but also from wandering bands of unwelcome human guerillas. No, the break from protocol was entirely on Igisha. He simply was not a happy camper, and I just happened to be in the wrong place at the wrong time.

I remember vividly that the Susa Group was spread out and foraging in a mountain meadow when we came upon them. I thought it was very considerate of Mother Nature to offer them this huge salad bowl in which to sit and casually eat their lunch. Led by the guides, we spread out as well, taking positions far enough from the gorillas so as not to disturb them while they dined. The clock began ticking. We had exactly one hour to observe and photograph our great ape cousins.

It's called *Kwita Izina*,

Rwanda's annual mountain gorilla naming ceremony. Each year since 2005, Rwandans have gathered in Volcanoes National Park to celebrate their country's newborn gorillas by giving names to individual animals and to thank the local communities, field researchers, veterinarians, research partners, and dedicated rangers and trackers who protect these magnificent creatures. Kwita Izina exemplifies Rwanda's commitment to responsible and sustainable ecotourism.

I was sitting in the middle of a thin trail that snaked its way through the alpine meadow, fiddling with my camera while small groups of gorillas sat at various points along the exposed slope, munching on crispy greens without any apparent care in the world. Igisha was alone and behind me; I had passed him only minutes before. He posed very proudly for several portrait shots and then watched me move on ahead. I failed to notice that after I passed him, he began to follow in my path. My first warning of his approach was the sound of vegetation yielding under the soles of his feet. I will never forget how soft the sound seemed for such a brute, how dark it became when his massive frame blocked the sun from my eyes, and how low I crouched, my head and torso bent over the camera with its long telephoto lens cradled against my belly to protect it from damage. And then, with merely a flick of his wrist, Igisha sent me toppling forward, head over heels in the most ungainly of somersaults, straight into a patch of wild celery. I'm not a large person, but I'm no lightweight either. One hundred eighty-five pounds of Konstant and camera gear were nothing in the ape's powerful hands.

Not a sound came from the silverback's mouth, but I could sense what he was thinking. Midway through my assisted gymnastics, I started to chuckle. This was no attack. The big guy never intended to bite me in the neck or hurt me in any way. I simply was blocking his path and he was just letting me know that that wasn't a very cool thing to do. Could he have spoken, I think he would have said, "Hey, I'm walkin' here! I'm walkin' here!" Imagine that, meeting a New York City gorilla on an African mountaintop. What were the odds?

Of course, no one got a photo of the incident, but a few members of our group did witness it and verified my account over a few beers around the campfire that night. I showered and changed before dinner, but made sure to bring my safari shirt to the storytelling session that followed. Igisha's dark fingerprints were clearly visible on the upper sleeve and would remain there until well after the trip ended. There came the point, however, where the stench of the shirt trumped the appeal of its story.

I should mention that I wasn't the only member of our group that Igisha manhandled that day. He also took exception to an Italian man who, like me, was prematurely gray. Perhaps Igisha perceived us as two lesser silverbacks, numbers five and six, on the climb to the top, a couple of weaklings he could push around. Whatever his motivation, the interactions were brief and essentially uneventful beyond their storytelling value.

IMPENDING YET UNEVENTFUL GORILLA-TOURIST ENCOUNTER, RWANDA, 2008

On an average day, nearly 100 tourists get up close and personal with Rwanda's mountain gorillas. The cost for a gorilla trekking permit in Rwanda these days is about $1,500, which buys each tourist no more than an hour's time with a gorilla group. If the price sounds exorbitant, it's important to understand that mountain gorilla tourism dollars support more than 100,000 jobs in Rwanda and account for more than 10% of the country's gross domestic product. These dollars not only pay for protecting the hundreds of gorillas that call Rwanda home but also help support wildlife conservation efforts in the country's other national parks and nature reserves.

Gorillas deserve their reputation as gentle giants and will continue to attract people from all over the world who come to see them in their natural habitat. Thanks to the work of dedicated wildlife conservationists over the past 40 to 50 years, the mountain gorilla population of Rwanda, Uganda, and the Democratic Republic of Congo has stabilized and is now

growing strongly, despite being surrounded by a dense human population and ongoing civil unrest in the region.

I must add a return trip to Rwanda to my bucket list, having recently received an update on the mountain gorillas of Volcanoes National Park from longtime friend and filmmaker Andy Young. Andy and his wife, Susan Todd, cofounders of Archipelago Films, are in the early stages of producing a wildlife documentary and have been following a large group of mountain gorillas in their daily travels through the Park. Their focus is the commitment of Rwandan field researchers, forest guards, tour guides and schoolchildren as they work together to protect and better understand these magnificent mountain gorillas. And would you like to guess which silverback gorilla is currently the front-runner for a lead role in this film production? That's right, my old buddy Igisha! It seems that he eventually left his old group to form a new one—some three dozen individuals strong—and is once and for all the top banana.

LESSON LEARNED:
There will be times—no matter how well prepared you might be for a situation—when circumstances may move beyond your control. Don't panic. Just take a deep breath, remain calm and rely on your instincts. Chances are that you'll be fine.

CHARLIE PERLITZ ON ONE OF OUR AFRICAN EXPEDITIONS, 2007

IN REMEMBRANCE

This trip to Rwanda was the last of three trips that Charlie Perlitz and I took together to see great apes in the wild. After visiting Borneo to see orangutans, we journeyed to see chimpanzees and lowland gorillas in Gabon, leaving only the mountain gorillas on his list. As you might have guessed, he didn't trek 3,000 feet up a mountain with me to meet the Susa Group but settled for a short walk from the tour bus to where a small group of mountain gorillas on the border of the National Park was trespassing on a farmer's field.

Charlie passed away on Halloween Day 2012 at the age of 81. During our travels together, he confided in me his plans for a bequest to the Houston Zoo. In his will, he left several million dollars to support the Zoo's wildlife conservation efforts around the world, including gorilla projects in the eastern Congo and an orangutan project in northeastern Borneo, as well as many other threatened species around the world. On behalf of all our wild brethren, I tip my hat and give sincere thanks to a good friend and a very caring, very generous man.

ADULT MALE WHITE RHINO, MKHAYA GAME RESERVE, SWAZILAND, 2014

FLYING ELEPHANT TURDS

Some people may think that this story is good,
others may think that it's rotten.
Those who don't like it can just push their nose
up the hole of an elephant's bottom.

"The Hole in the Elephant's Bottom"
19th Century British Music Hall Song

Although the title suggests that this is a story about elephants, it's really about rhinos. It just begins with elephant poop.

"Incoming!!!" It would have been nice had someone issued such a warning, but no one did. The three intended targets in the back of the bus were pleased to see that the projectile was going to miss its mark.

Whap!!!

The dried elephant turd cleared the open window and caught me just above the right temple, a sensitive and vulnerable part of the skull, and not a place one would choose to be hit with an object of any kind. Raucous laughter from the three clowns seated behind me was almost immediate. Luckily, the turd wasn't fresh, but rather sun-dried and now largely devoid of water weight.

On impact, it exploded into a powdery cloud of digested leaves, twigs, and grasses, coating the upper half of my body and leaving me smelling like a horse barn. The two women seated in front of me flinched. Behind me, Moe, Larry and Curly rocked back and forth, held their bellies and laughed even louder.

My right arm shot up reflexively, much too late to thwart the surprise attack. I could only hope to shield myself from the next round. Who the hell was tossing elephant turds at the bus anyway? I was one of several dozen biologists who had been invited to Kruger National Park in March 2014 for a special conference and workshop focused on rhino poaching. Those of us on the bus had spent several hours that morning in meetings and were being treated to a field trip, an opportunity to commune with nature and stretch our legs—some well-deserved R & R.

I shook the debris from my hair, wiped my neck and shirt, and immediately began thinking about the long shower I would enjoy when we returned to our rooms. Then I glared out the open window at my attacker. The culprit raised both his arms high in the air, palms up and outstretched. He cocked his head to one side—the universal sign for "Sorry man, that wasn't supposed to happen!"—and managed the most anemic apologetic smile. In his mind, I was just collateral damage since he was really aiming for the three laughing hyenas behind me. I shook the dust from my hair again and nodded my head to confirm that no real harm was done. We both understood that the incident could be settled diplomatically, sorted out later over a beer or two and a good laugh as well.

Such was my introduction to Mick Reilly. Mick hails from the Kingdom of Eswatini, a small landlocked neighbor of South Africa, previously known as the Kingdom of Swaziland. His trip to Kruger National Park was a hell of a lot shorter than mine. Kruger is home to the world's largest population of white rhinos (more than three thousand at last count) and several hundred

MICK REILLY WITH WHITE RHINOS, MKHAYA GAME RESERVE, SWAZILAND, 2014

black rhinos. However, the Park has also been a global epicenter of rhino poaching, with an average of one or more animals slaughtered every day for their horns in recent years. Hired as the International Rhino Foundation's program director in 2012, I was a newbie to the global rhino conservation community. My job was to help raise funds for anti-poaching programs in both Africa and Asia. Mick and the dozens of other participants at the Kruger workshop all risk their lives on a daily basis to protect threatened wildlife, and they had gathered together to compare notes.

Game rangers in southern Africa battle against an unending assault of wildlife poaching. Most of the poachers enter Kruger National Park from Mozambique along the 250-mile shared border with South Africa. Protecting that border requires well-armed, well-trained teams of rangers and their canine companions. One of the Kruger squads, including a Belgian Malinois named Killer, gave us a small demonstration of their work. Here's how the pursuit of poachers might unfold. A

ANTI-POACHING TRAINING SESSION, KRUGER NATIONAL PARK, 2014

ranger spots a suspicious group of people somewhere in the Park and radios base camp to alert the rest of the squad. A pilot jumps into the cockpit of a helicopter as a couple of rangers grab their automatic weapons and a tracking dog, in this case, Killer. The team hops aboard. In a matter of minutes, the helicopter lifts off with one of the rangers precariously perched on the landing skid—yes, *outside* of the cockpit—scanning the terrain for movement. Once spotted, the copter closes in on the poachers, touching down at a safe distance. Killer and his trainer leap from the cockpit and the chase is on with Killer quickly outpacing and restraining his quarry.

After the conference, Mick invited several colleagues and me to spend a few days with his family. Years before he was born, back in the 1930s and 1940s, his homeland's wildlife had been systematically slaughtered. Animals were gunned down with machine guns and poisoned at waterholes. By the early 1960s, the small African nation was no longer home to elephants, rhinos, hippos, buffalo, lions, giraffes or zebras. All had been wiped out by poaching. In response, Mick's dad Ted, with the support of King Sobhuza II, converted the family farm in Mlilwane into a wildlife sanctuary. In 1964, the King proclaimed the new sanctuary a national protected area, and Swaziland's Big Game Parks was born, a nonprofit trust to be managed by the Reilly family.

Our group stayed at Big Game Parks' Mkhaya Game Reserve—a very enchanted place. Visitors stay in stone-walled, thatch-roofed cottages open to the elements and the occasional wandering critter. Small frogs guarded my shower stall when I wasn't using it. One morning, an inquisitive bird felt the need to inspect the contents of the pockets of a shirt I had placed on the nightstand the night before. And my stay certainly would not have been complete without a bat or two whisking through the room in the middle of the night. The tiny insects that clung to the mosquito netting draped over my bed were just too tempting.

I recently learned that Killer passed away following a lengthy illness. A few years after I met him, he received the PDSA Gold Medal for Courage—the nonhuman animal version of the United Kingdom's esteemed George Cross. The honor recognized Killer's dedicated service to protect endangered rhinos. His tracking skills led to the arrest of more than 100 poachers. Killer protected his handler when he was under heavy fire, and through it all, he undoubtedly saved the lives of innumerable rhinos.

Sitting around the campfire after dinner, Ted Reilly, the patriarch and our host, entertained his guests with stories of family adventures through the decades. The Reillys are largely responsible for reintroducing all the species that had been exterminated in their country. White rhinos were returned

TED REILLY INTRODUCES GUESTS TO A WHITE RHINO MOTHER AND CALF,
MKHAYA GAME RESERVE, SWAZILAND, 2014

in 1965, black rhinos in 1986. And thanks to intensive anti-poaching efforts, only a handful of rhinos have been lost over the last few decades. Strong government support from the very top and a zero-tolerance approach from law enforcement officials have been key to this success. The accomplishment is even more significant when you consider that this tiny country is sandwiched between what Mick and his father rightly describe as the "two hottest rhino poaching spots on the globe."

In the reserve one morning, Ted pointed to a couple of white rhinos just off the dirt track ahead of us, a mother and her calf. He pulled up beside them and introduced us to the adult female, Mbali. She came to Mkhaya years before as a young orphan, her own mother shot by poachers. The Reillys hand-raised her, so she's tolerant of people. We each stepped out of the vehicle, patted Mbali's thick hide, and scratched the tender skin behind her ears, just like you would the family dog. Her male calf, Mvelo, who she raised on her own, was only slightly less social.

TWO SCORPIOS MEET, MKHAYA GAME RESERVE, SWAZILAND, 2014
PHOTO COURTESY OF MICK REILLY

Mick took us on a game drive that afternoon. We stopped to watch a giraffe feeding from the tops of acacia trees. While we watched, it stopped eating abruptly, looked off into the distance, slowly lowered its head and moved away. Mick thought something might be amiss. He pulled the vehicle to a stop, reached behind the driver's seat and pulled out a small automatic rifle. Motioning that we should stay put, he walked off into the bush in the direction the giraffe had taken. We waited in silence, anticipating a burst of gunfire, but none followed. Several minutes later, Mick reappeared. A false alarm.

A highlight for me during our visit to Mkhaya was meeting Scorpio and Margot, two anti-poaching shepherd dogs that Mick was training. For protection, the training program's "poacher" wore a helmet and a thickly-padded suit, looking more like a cross between a man from outer space and the Pillsbury Doughboy than a criminal. His appearance didn't faze Margot, however, who Mick taught to attack any threatening character

MARGOT ATTACKS A "POACHER," MKHAYA GAME RESERVE, SWAZILAND, 2014

on command. The dog learned to latch on and not release until the poacher was subdued. It couldn't have been any fun to be on the receiving end of Margot's attack, even protected by a heavily-padded suit. In fact, I'll bet it hurt a hell of a lot more than being hit in the head with an elephant turd.

LESSON LEARNED:
Anti-poaching dogs and their handlers are an excellent example of teamwork between two species that help save other species. I never cease to be amazed by the loyalty and dedication of our canine companions.

ANDATU'S MOTHER, RATU, THE SUMATRAN RHINO SANCTUARY, 2012

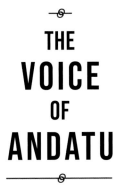

THE
VOICE
OF
ANDATU

The Beast had a head like that of a rhinoceros, only there were five eyes in its face. There were five long arms growing out of its body, and it also had five long, slim legs. Thick, woolly hair covered every part of it, and a more dreadful-looking monster could not be imagined.

Frank Baum, *The Wizard of Oz* (1900)

Ratu, one of three adult females at the Sumatran Rhino Sanctuary, just finished her breakfast and was heading back into the forest as our vehicle pulled up to her enclosure. March of 2012 saw my first visit to the Sanctuary and I hoped to get a few photos of her. She was pregnant and due to give birth in just a few months. Her baby would be the first of its kind to be born at the Sanctuary, in fact, the first to be born in captivity in all of Indonesia. Given that scientists believed only a few hundred Sumatran rhinos survived in the wild at that time, the impending birth was a much-anticipated event and well worth celebrating.

Our vehicle came to a stop, I hopped out and made a beeline for the fence, barely keeping pace with Ratu's retreat into the forest. I poked the camera lens through the wire in the fence, zoomed in, and focused on her butt as it disappeared into the foliage. Damn! Just not quick enough! Acting on reflex, I pursed my lips and drew in a quick breath of air, making the same sound I use to

RATU, POSING IN HER ENCLOSURE, THE SUMATRAN RHINO SANCTUARY, 2012

call my dog. I don't think the sound has a name. It's somewhere between a whistle and a kiss and seems to work well in getting the attention of many kinds of animals including, I discovered, rhinos. Ratu halted in her tracks, her posterior filling the camera frame.

Very slowly, she began to back out of the forest and swivel her head in my direction. Before I knew it, she was offering a profile view. Then she took a few steps closer and did a full body turn, a move she must have learned at the Sumatran Rhino Modeling Academy. I shot dozens of images.

Three months later, Ratu gave birth to Andatu. His name is a combination of his father's, Andalas, who was born at the Cincinnati Zoo in 2001, and his mother's, who had been found wandering around a nearby Sumatran village in 2005. In addition to Andalas and Ratu, two other female rhinos, Rosa and Bina, lived at the Sanctuary when I first visited in 2012. Both were also rescued from similar situations as Ratu, but neither had yet bred.

TWO-YEAR-OLD ANDATU IN HIS FOREST ENCLOSURE, 2014

The Sumatran rhino is the smallest and hairiest of the world's five remaining rhino species: the white, black, greater one-horned, Javan and Sumatran. Both the white rhino and the black rhino live in Africa. Their names are misnomers. The white rhino isn't white and the black rhino isn't black; both are brownish-gray. The white rhino is the largest of the five species, with large males weighing as much as 6,000 pounds. Topping the scale at 3,000 pounds, its cousin, the black rhino, is the second smallest. Both sport two long horns, which make them prime targets for poachers.

Three rhino species live in Asia. The greater one-horned or Indian rhinoceros makes its home in India and Nepal, while the Javan and Sumatran rhinos are now found only in Indonesia. In past decades, both Javan and Sumatran rhinos also roamed mainland Asia's tropical forests. Their historic ranges, in fact, once extended from Southeast Asia to the foothills of the Himalayas. At two to three tons, greater one-horned rhinos rival Africa's white rhino in size. Populations of both species were reduced to the low hundreds at the turn of the 20th century. Still, their numbers have rebounded significantly thanks to relentless, long-term action against poaching. More than 4,000 greater one-horned rhinos are now alive and the number of white rhinos is close to 16,000.

The Javan rhino, like its Indian cousin, has a single horn. It is found today only on the island of Java in a single protected area, the Ujung Kulon National Park. It once also roamed the neighboring island of Sumatra, but the last individual there probably met its fate in the 1930s or 1940s. The last Javan rhino documented on mainland Asia was shot and killed in Vietnam in 2010.

Oddly enough,

the closest relative of the Sumatran rhino is the extinct, two-horned woolly rhinoceros that roamed the vast Siberian tundra during the Ice Age tens of thousands of years ago. The arrival of humans wielding spears and clubs may have swung the initial blow to the woolly rhino's eventual decline and demise, but scientists now believe that a warming planet—climate change—was the death knell for this species.

The average Javan rhino weighs between one and two tons, near the middle of the rhino weight range. An estimated and stable population of more than 70 individuals continues to hang on by a very slender thread on the extreme western tip of Java. I've been to Ujung Kulon National Park three times, twice to lead tours and once specifically to search for this elusive creature, but I have yet to see a living specimen. I've encountered Javan rhino tracks, wallows (rhino bathtubs), poop, and shrubs on which it has fed, and I've smelled its urine along the trail, but that's it.

I've also never seen a wild Sumatran rhino, only the handful at the Sanctuary and one at the Cincinnati Zoo. A full-grown male

GREATER ONE-HORNED RHINO, KAZIRANGA NATIONAL PARK, INDIA, 2014

might weigh as much as a ton, but that would be unusual. Like the two African rhinos and their extinct woolly relative, the Sumatran rhino has two horns, but they are very small. Its fate now rests with the animals remaining in two Sumatran national parks: Way Kambas and Gunung Leuser. Occasional reports of isolated individuals continue to emerge from Indonesian Borneo and even from distant Myanmar but, as far as I know, no concrete conservation action has been undertaken in either region. Due to ongoing habitat loss and poaching, the total population of this species is estimated at less than 100 animals.

The Sumatran Rhino Sanctuary is inside Way Kambas National Park on the southern tip of the island. Visitors to Way Kambas can tour the Sanctuary and meet its rhinos face-to-face. Each animal has access to several acres of tropical forest and receives daily care from a team of keepers and veterinarians. A diet of fresh fruits and vegetables from the market is supplemented with a variety of vegetation that the keepers collect from the surrounding forest, as well as what the animals can forage in

WAY KAMBAS NATIONAL PARK RHINO PROTECTION UNIT, SUMATRA, 2012

their spacious enclosures. Beyond the facility boundaries, roving Rhino Protection Units monitor the status of wild Sumatran rhinos, elephants and tigers.

Andatu's birth on June 12, 2012, was celebrated throughout Indonesia. Shortly afterward, the folks at the International Rhino Foundation decided he should have his own Facebook page, just like his mom, dad and the other rhinos at the Sanctuary. Given the youngster's unique history, my colleagues at the Foundation and I saw no problem with the little guy pushing the envelope just a bit. His Facebook posts could be engaging as well as informative. They might be more conversational and reveal how he perceives the world. We also thought it would be best if Andatu communicated in a "first-rhino voice" when sharing posts with his human friends. People should enjoy conversing with him, if only electronically.

That I volunteered to be Andatu's voice should be no surprise. My instructions were simple: "Knock yourself out!" So, for his inaugural post, little Andatu shared a photo of his mother's humongous butt. His message was pretty straightforward:

"Here's what I get to look at every day as I follow Mom through the forest. Welcome to my world!"

For the next year and a half, Andatu gave all his social media friends an inside look at the life of a young Sumatran rhinoceros. He explained that his name, in addition to being a combination of his father's and mother's, was also an Indonesian term that means a "Gift from God." Andatu informed the world of how fast he was growing, reaching 100 pounds—almost double his birth weight—in just one month. He complained that his head was too big and heavy, and how he was exhausted by the end of the day just carrying it around. He asked animal-loving actress Betty White and basketball star Yao Ming to friend him. He introduced the world to the keepers, the veterinarians who cared for him, and the rangers who patrolled the surrounding forests. Andatu directed all his friends to the International Rhino Foundation website, inviting them to learn 25 Things You Might Not Know about Rhinos.

I must thank my good friend and communications guru, Kelly Russo, for managing the Voice of Andatu. She and I had worked together closely at the Houston Zoo for several years. It was Kelly's idea for Andatu to round up 1,000 friends by World Rhino Day, September 2012, a feat he accomplished at a mere three months of age.

News of Andatu's birth spread quickly around the world, eventually reaching the elementary school students of PS 107, the John W. Kimball Learning Center in Brooklyn, New York. The children were so excited they invited me to their school to speak about Andatu's role as an ambassador for wildlife conservation in Indonesia. Learning about Andatu inspired the fifth graders to launch a special project for their Beast Relief program. They decided to write a book titled *One Special Rhino: The Story of Andatu*. The students divided themselves into teams: one to research, one to write, another to fact-check, and so on.

TWO-YEAR-OLD ANDATU, PRESENTED WITH HIS BIOGRAPHY, 2014

They asked me to review their work prior to publication.

PTA mom and author/journalist Katherine Eban coordinated my work with the students. Ultimately, all 85 fifth graders participated. Their book wound up being featured in *National Geographic Kids*, *Scholastic Magazine* and the *National Geographic Kids 2016 Almanac*. Dr. Jane Goodall wrote the introduction and received an autographed copy from the four principal authors, thanking her for the endorsement. I then had the exceptional privilege of hand-carrying copies halfway around the world—a few for the staff at the Sumatran Rhino Sanctuary and one for Andatu himself. The occasion provided the ultimate Kodak moment.

One Special Rhino was a first for the students of PS 107. They donated proceeds from sales to the International Rhino Foundation for Sumatran rhino conservation. On its heels came *One Special Elephant: The Story of Penelope Petunia*, which helped raise funds for forest elephant field research in the Central African Republic; *One Special Orangutan: The Story of Budi*, which helped support the rescue and rehabilitation of orphaned orangutans in Borneo; and *One Special Tiger: The Story of Zalushka*, a fundraiser for similar efforts on behalf of Siberian tigers in the Russian Far East.

PS 107 is a very special school indeed. And its students, parents and teachers can take great pride in their efforts. Children's books written by children to help save endangered species show how each of us can make a difference, no matter how big, how small, how young, or how old.

LESSON LEARNED:
Never underestimate the power of a child with a purpose. Childhood enthusiasm can be electric, contagious and "through the roof"—a veritable Fountain of Youth for us old-timers.

GREATER ONE-HORNED RHINOCEROS (OR INDIAN RHINOCEROUS)
KAZIRANGA NATIONAL PARK, INDIA, 2014

NANNETTE'S TECHNICOLOR RHINOCEROS

The rhino is a homely beast,
for human eyes he's not a feast.
Farewell, farewell, you old rhinoceros,
I'll stare at something less prepoceros.

Ogden Nash, "The Rhinoceros"

In 2015, Nannette agreed to a quilting project that was as unique as it was inspirational: a quilt celebrating the 500th anniversary of Albrecht Dürer's *The Rhinoceros*, a world-famous woodcut. Only a few of the German artist's original black-and-white prints have survived, some featured in museum collections and others fetching the high six figures at auction. Nannette created her interpretation of Dürer's work as a brightly colored quilt for a special auction at the Houston Zoo. The top bid for her handiwork would go entirely to rhino conservation. If you'll allow me to delve briefly into some ancient history, the inspiration for her project will become apparent.

In the days of the Roman Empire, in the first century following the birth of Christ, a naturalist known as Pliny the Elder declared that elephants and rhinoceroses were mortal enemies. He offered no evidence, but no one questioned his expert opinion. A millennium and a half later, King Manuel I of Portugal decided to test Pliny's theory. The king had been given a rhinoceros by one of his governors, Alfonso de Albuquerque. Governor de Albuquerque ruled over Portugal's latest land grab in what is now known as India. His gift to the king was Ganda, a young, female greater one-horned rhino that lived in—as in *inside*—the home of a sea captain who delivered her to her new owner in 1515.

Ganda departed the port city of Goa on a cold January morning, bound for Lisbon. She spent three months aboard the *Nossa Senhora d'Ajuda* (Our Lady of Hope), which transported her southwest around Africa's Cape of Good Hope and then north across the eastern Atlantic Ocean, the reverse of Portuguese explorer Vasco de Gama's infamous route. Ganda was the first rhino seen in Europe since the Romans brought rhinos to the Colisseum for bloodsports. For most 16th-century Europeans, the rhinoceros was a mythical beast, believed by some to be the legendary unicorn. That made Ganda's arrival an extraordinary event indeed.

In Lisbon, Ganda was kept in the king's menagerie at the Ribeira Palace. Having read Pliny the Elder's works, Manuel I decided to test the premise that rhinos and elephants are eternal foes. A servant tried to introduce Ganda to one of the king's elephants, housed next door at the Estaus Palace. As the servant led the young rhino toward the elephant, its leg tethered to a post by an iron chain, the pachyderm spooked. It snapped its chain and bolted out of the yard. Those present must have wondered, "Could Pliny be right?"

Ganda was a national celebrity during her time in Portugal. Among her visitors were artists who sketched this strange new beast. One sent his work to a young German Renaissance artist by the name of Albrecht Dürer. Without ever laying eyes on a live rhinoceros, Dürer used his friend's sketch to create his own version of Ganda. What's amazing to me is that his secondhand version has survived for centuries as perhaps the world's most

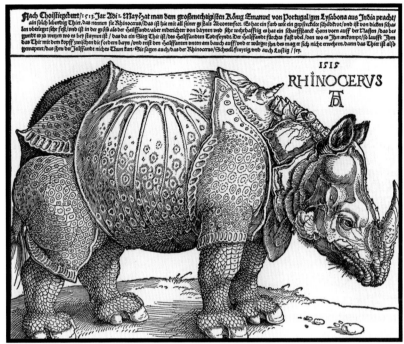

THE RHINOCEROS
WOODCUT BY ALBRECHT DÜRER (1515)

iconic image of a rhinoceros. Critics of his work point out that *The Rhinoceros* is not entirely accurate anatomically, but c'mon, he had no option other than to work from notes. I mean, at a time when most people probably still believed that the world was flat, why vilify a guy because he thought rhinos might be iron plated?

After spending less than a year in Lisbon, Ganda embarked on her second sea voyage. Along with a cargo of silver and spices, she was loaded aboard a ship bound for Rome since King Manuel I decided to regift her to Pope Leo X. It was not an uncommon practice of the day to curry favor with the papacy by giving exotic creatures as presents. Sadly, Ganda's second voyage was to be her last. Shortly after her ship set sail from Marseilles, it encountered a severe storm and sank with Ganda on deck. Eventually, her carcass washed up along the French

Riviera, where her hide was removed and sent back to Lisbon. Taxidermists restored her as best they could and then sent her to Rome.

I saw my first wild greater one-horned rhino in India's northeastern state of Assam in January 2014. On a densely foggy morning in Kaziranga National Park, I braced against the damp chill while sitting on an elephant that apparently did not get Pliny's memo about rhinos being mortal enemies. Kaziranga holds the world's largest population of greater one-horned rhinos—more than two thousand individuals. Kaziranga also boasts high densities of tigers and wild water buffaloes, neither of which is to be taken for granted when there's nothing but air between your body and theirs. The rhinos and tigers are quite capable of hiding from you in the tall, aptly-named elephant grass until the very last moment. Amazingly, I felt quite safe, despite being in what might be considered a precarious position on my howdah, a seat that can accommodate two people, in this case, me and a trusty mahout "at the wheel." I imagined myself as Mowgli riding atop his elephant friend Hathi, the Master of the Jungle. Should my nemesis, Shere Khan the Tiger, be lurking in the fog, I readied my camera to capture his image. Then, the mahout slowed our elephant to a halt, not wanting to trample over the rhinoceros that had magically appeared in front of us, calmly munching its vegetarian breakfast. There was no tension in the air, no twitching of elephant or rhino muscles. My elephant stood stock-still and, in less than a minute, was joined by several other tuskers and their riders, our congregation forming a semicircle of the world's largest land animals around the second largest.

By midmorning, we observed several dozen rhinos in the eastern section of Kaziranga where wildlife has been habituated to tourist-bearing elephants. That was not yet the case in the area's central section and may still be a long-term goal in the western portion, where irritated rhinos are apt to charge and

THE CHASE IS ON, KAZIRANGA NATIONAL PARK, INDIA, 2014

chase vehicles. Around the campfire that evening, the National Park's newly-appointed director explained the situation. He told us that the rhinos of western Kaziranga were relatively new to the ecotourism experience and could still pose a threat. Equally dangerous were the hundreds of wild water buffalo that shared their habitat. In fact, stirring the embers with a stick, the director confessed that the water buffalo were responsible for one or more ranger injuries—even deaths—each year. I stared into the fire and spoke without diverting my gaze, "Don't you think that's something someone should have told us yesterday?" In hindsight, it's probably best that they didn't say a word.

Fast forward two years and I'm sitting by Nan at the Houston Zoo's 9th Annual Conservation Gala. She's staring at her cell phone and the folks across the table are eyeing theirs as well. It's not a hard and fast rule, but my wife and I discourage the use of cell phones at the table. You can make a phone call later or take it to another room. No Google search is so urgent, no app so cool, or selfie so important that it can't wait until later, and it

The future

of the greater one-horned rhino hinges on rebuilding populations that have declined or disappeared due to poaching. With more effective protection measures now in place, translocation has become an important conservation tool. The increasing rhino population of Kaziranga National Park is critical to re-establishing this species in Assam's Manas National Park and ensuring its survival in Orang National Park and the Pobitora Wildlife Sanctuary.

certainly shouldn't compete with good old-fashioned dinner conversation. The Zoo gala, however, was a different situation entirely. Nan's eyes, as well as mine, were glued to her phone as our salads were served. We watched the numbers change, the bids growing higher and higher as fellow diners competed against one another for auction items. Several were bidding for the honor of owning Nan's quilted version of Dürer's *The Rhinoceros*. Nan's rendition of the original is a rainbow of brilliantly colored fabrics, ornamented with buttons and beads, and custom-stitched in fine detail to accentuate the rhino's unusual armor-like hide. The quilt took her two years to finish. Dürer completed his woodcut in 1515, so we set the opening bid for Nan's quilt at $1,515. The silent auction would last only five minutes more, with the bids having just hit the $2,000 mark.

We ate our salad and watched our phones as the numbers rose. One of our table companions was in the running for the quilt, having programmed incremental bid increases of $50 into the auction app on his phone. The waitstaff cleared our salad plates and had just begun serving our entrees when the auction's ending bell rang. Okay, there was no bell, but it was easy to imagine one. At the close, a gentleman at the far end of the event tent bid $3,000 and took home Nan's quilt to hang on his wall.

NANNETTE'S PRIZE-WINNING QUILT AT THE NATIONAL QUILT EXTRAVAGANZA, 2016
PHOTO COURTESY OF HELEN MARIE MARSHALL

Rhino conservation was the theme of the 2015 gala, which meant that a significant portion of the money raised in table sales and auction proceeds would support rhino conservation projects in Africa and Asia. We raised more than $1 million that evening, about 20 percent of the Zoo's conservation budget for the year. I thought back to 2003 when Rick Barongi and I first began building the Naturally Wild conservation program. The budget was a mere $100,000. What a difference a decade makes!

LESSON LEARNED:
We should never doubt that each and every one of us has the ability, the connections, and the opportunities to make a difference, and it certainly doesn't hurt to have some hidden talent as well.

BLUE AT HOME AND IN HIS ELEMENT, PENNSYLVANIA, 2015

BLUE

*If aliens are watching us through telescopes, they're going to think
the dogs are the leaders of the planet. If you see two life forms,
one of them's making a poop, the other one's carrying it for him,
who would you assume is in charge?*

Jerry Seinfeld

Somehow, I managed to survive for more than 20 years
without a dog in the house. Kilo, my college pooch, was
adopted by my parents in 1973, and it wasn't until 1995 that
my family rescued one from a local shelter. Nan, the kids and
I walked a line of chain-link pens holding dogs of every color,
shape and size. All but one pleaded their cases, barking as we
passed them. A lone black-and-white dog just sat quietly in the
far corner of its pen and slowly wagged its tail when we made
eye contact. A small sign on the door to her pen made it clear
that this was her last chance for adoption. If not selected, she'd
be history 24 hours later. We all looked at one another after
reading the sign and knew there was no leaving without her.

That was Maggie. Her papers identified her as an eight-month-
old border collie mix, but 12 years later we found out that the
folks at the shelter were mistaken. I was in Montana visiting the
wolves at Yellowstone and staying at the nearby Elk Meadow
Ranch. The ranch manager was giving me a tour of the spread
when we came upon two black-and-white dogs out back in
their pens. One looked very much like Maggie.

"Looks like you have a border collie mix just like mine," I
remarked, pointing to the dog on the left. The ranch manager

MAGGIE RELAXING ON THE BACKYARD DECK, PENNSYLVANIA, 2003

smiled, prepared to correct my mistake without embarrassing me, "That's a purebred Karelian bear dog. The border collie, the one on the right, takes care of the herding. The Karelian protects our cattle from grizzlies and wolves." A second, more scrutinizing look confirmed the subtle differences, and I realized that there very well might be a few Karelian bear dog genes hidden somewhere in Maggie's family tree.

The breed, which I had never heard of before, hails from Karelia, a region of lakes, forests and peat bogs that has changed hands between Russia and Nordic countries for centuries. The Finns, in particular, take great pride in the Karelian bear dog's fearless nature and skill for hunting bear, moose, wolf, lynx and wild boar. An Animal Planet Dogs 101 episode describes these dogs as being "kind of wolfie." The episode also explains that the breed was almost driven to extinction during World War II, discourages people from confining these canines to small quarters, and gives Karelians an A+ in the health department. The program warns, however, that rigorous training might be required to socialize them.

MOM AND BLUE, BUSHKILL FALLS, PENNSYLVANIA, 2012

Maggie lived up to the breed's reputation but never had any socialization problems. She was exceptionally tolerant of other dogs and our three cats and gave us 14 years of loyalty and devotion. I had total confidence in Maggie and would walk her off-leash, whether up and down a busy street or out in the woods. No matter where we went, there wasn't a day that went by without someone commenting, "Nice dog!"

After Maggie died, Nan and I didn't waste any time adopting our next rescue. Within a couple of weeks, our daughter Melanie found the soon-to-be canine member of the family online, the way everything's done these days. She found a certified Karelian bear dog rescue about an hour's drive away, knowing that we had developed a particular fondness for this breed. So, just as we did when we adopted Maggie, the whole family jumped in the car and went to have a look. We wound up on a small ranch in neighboring Chester County and were introduced to a young Karelian mix by the name of Sprocket. I remember asking myself, "Why would anyone name their dog Sprocket?" But it

BLUE, FORT WASHINGTON STATE PARK, PENNSYLVANIA, 2018

didn't matter. He was one handsome pooch. His one ice-blue eye told of some Siberian husky blood. His markings, however, were more Karelian than husky, which also really didn't matter since our meeting was love at first sight.

Sprocket was off-leash at the opposite end of a large field, standing next to a pony (the rescue found homes for horses as well). The owner let us in through a gate and called him. He bounded across the field and into the arms of his new family. He nuzzled and licked us as if he'd returned home after surviving months wandering in the wilderness. Yes, this dog was coming home with us. On the ride back, we bandied about dozens of possible names (Sprocket was definitely history), calling out each one and noting our new pup's reaction. "Klondike!" Nothing. "Tundra!" Nada. "Bear!" drew a faint head tilt, but it was "Blue"—the distinctive color of his right eye—that really perked up his ears. So Blue it was.

The very next morning, I took Blue to Fort Washington State Park for our first walk in the woods together. Leaving the car windows open on that warm July day may not have been the best idea in the world. I was the second one in the car to notice a white-tailed deer browsing at the side of the road. Blue saw it first. The deer must have noticed the large dog staring at it

from the open car window because it got spooked and took off up the hill. In the snap of a finger, Blue's hind legs flexed and his front legs shot upward, launching him straight out the window like a bat out of hell. He hit the ground running, racing after his prey, rapidly gaining ground. I pulled the truck to a stop and could only sit there and watch the pursuit as my new dog and his quarry both disappeared over the hill.

The next five minutes seemed like 50. When I finally saw Blue's silhouette coming back down the slope, I breathed a deep sigh of relief. He was moving quite a bit slower in his return, as well as shaking his head from side to side. When he got closer, I noticed a few drops of blood dripping from his muzzle, nothing that looked serious, but very likely evidence that he indeed caught up to the deer and took a hoof to the face as a reward for his efforts. I opened the passenger side door and he hopped back into the truck, no coaxing necessary. Since it appeared that he had already been punished for his transgression, I just looked at him, shook my head and laughed. My work as a dog owner and trainer was clearly cut out for me.

That was in 2010. Blue just turned 14. Since he joined the family, Blue and I probably have hiked more than 12,000 miles together. We've come to know the trails of many of eastern Pennsylvania's state and county parks, nature reserves and wildlife

The Karelian

bear dog is an important ally in the effort to reduce human-wildlife conflicts in northern wilderness regions. This breed, as its name might imply, is called upon to haze bears that wander too close to populated areas, creating an unpleasant experience for the bruins and conditioning them to steer clear of humans. Karelian bear dogs are routinely employed for such service in the United States, Canada and Japan.

BLUE, NOCKAMIXON STATE PARK, PENNSYLVANIA, 2015

sanctuaries like the backs of my hands and the bottoms of his paws. There isn't a day Blue walks with me when someone doesn't comment on what a beautiful or handsome dog he is. Literally! In fact, it usually happens two or three times on any given walk. Cars have even come to a stop in traffic just so the driver can compliment Blue's good looks.

BLUE, WISSAHICKON CREEK, PENNSYLVANIA, 2015

The ladies seem particularly fond of him. "Hey, handsome!" they'll call out, to which I'm quick to respond, "I assume you're speaking to my dog?" That never fails to elicit a laugh and a smile. Nan calls Blue my "chick magnet" and I take advantage of his superpowers to engage in conversation any chance I get. Nine out of 10 folks have never heard of a Karelian bear dog, so I've got a great story in my pocket and I'm happy to tell it at the drop of a hat.

Many of the kids we meet along the trail are convinced that Blue is a wolf. One child asked his father, "Dad, is that a werewolf?" Dad offered up, "No, it's just a regular wolf. Werewolves are make-believe."

In 2014, I invited Dr. Jane Goodall to join Blue and me for a stroll through Wissahickon Valley Park. Jane was lecturing locally and staying at a nearby hotel. She and I had met several times through the years at presentations and wildlife conservation events and became friends. Jane loves dogs as much as or more than I do, so she didn't hesitate to accept the invitation. However, her schedule quickly became swamped, forcing her to cancel our walk in the Wissahickon. I proposed a Plan B. "If you can't join me for a hike, how would you like to spend 15 minutes with Blue?" Jane didn't miss a beat, "I want at least a half hour with

DR. JANE GOODALL AND BLUE, WAYNE, PENNSYLVANIA, 2014

Blue! You and he can come to see me at my hotel. If they give you any trouble at the front desk, just tell them that Blue is my therapy dog."

So that afternoon, Nan, Blue and I jumped in the car, took a ride to Jane's hotel and did just as she instructed. The man at the front desk had no issue with Blue going up to the room, but I explained to him that Blue was Dr. Goodall's therapy dog anyway, knowing that Blue would appreciate the recognition. For the next hour, he sat on the couch beside Jane, perfectly content to be petted and stroked.

Mid-stroke through Blue's thick, soft fur, Jane looked over at me and asked, "Bill, have you heard of an Israeli primatologist by the name of Itai Roffman?" I hadn't. "He's begun to study the chimpanzees of Mali, which live in a harsh, almost desert-like environment, quite unlike their habitats in the tropical forests of Gombe and other parts of Africa." I had never been to Mali and knew very little about the chimpanzees there. "It's bound to be a very interesting project, and I'd like to help raise some seed

money for Itai. He also plans to help create better conditions for rescued chimpanzees at the national zoo. And, he's keen to establish a Mali chapter of Roots & Shoots," a signature international program of the Jane Goodall Institute.

Jane went on to explain that Itai had already begun working with local villagers, assessing their attitudes toward wild primates and trying to determine how best to obtain long-term community commitments for their protection. It sounded like a very ambitious and worthwhile project. Not needing to noodle the concept further, my reply was straightforward, "Itai should apply for a grant from the Mohamed bin Zayed Species Conservation Fund. I serve as an advisor on mammal projects and think that a proposal of this nature would be worth consideration." Some months later, Itai submitted a request for support and received sufficient funding to embark upon his efforts in Mali. Years later, his initiatives continue to make a significant impact on wildlife conservation and have received ongoing support. In addition, in July 2022, the Jane Goodall Institute announced its first branch in Israel. Its home: The Max Stern Yezreel Valley College. Its codirector: Itai Roffman.

So Jane got her half hour with Blue, I got to spend quality time with someone I've admired since I was a young boy, and I was introduced to a new colleague (whom I look forward to meeting someday). And I now have good reason to visit a new country and join the people of Mali in protecting their precious natural heritage. I also hope that someday Jane, Blue and I get a chance to take that special walk in the Wissahickon.

LESSON LEARNED:
I believe humans and dogs share what's known as "pack mentality," a trait that can bring together individuals with similar interests and complementary talents.

RIO, A MALE JAGUAR, RIO CUIABÁ, BRAZIL, 2022

99 JAGUARS

God decided to make man because the jaguar already existed.

Alan Rabinowitz
Jaguar: One Man's Struggle to Save Jaguars in the Wild (1987)

Rafael leaned forward in his seat, arms extended and hands held apart just enough to hold a small watermelon. "Its head was this big and almost this close to me! I had my revolver in hand, mainly as a precaution for any cranky buffalo I might startle, but never considered shooting. When the jaguar first charged, I think it could only see my bottom half through the thick vegetation, probably just up to my belt. It wasn't until the animal got close and looked up that it could see my face, that I was a man. When it realized that, it stopped dead in its tracks and quickly vanished into the forest."

At six feet, two inches tall, Rafael Hoogesteijn's figure is imposing, apparently enough to give even an adult jaguar—South America's largest carnivore—pause. Sitting across the table from me in a hotel dining room in the small Brazilian city of Cuiabá, Rafael effortlessly entertained me and the other guests as we awaited dinner. Our host, born in Venezuela, received his veterinary training in the late 1970s, followed by a Master's degree in Wildlife Management and Conservation from the University of Florida at Gainesville. He now works for the US-based organization Panthera, founded in 2006 and dedicated to the survival of all of the world's wild cat species and their habitats. Stationed in the Pantanal region of Brazil's Mato Grosso state, Rafael is the director of Panthera's Jofre Velho Conservation Ranch, a demonstration project where local cattle ranchers can learn how to safely maintain their herds in the realm of the region's robust jaguar population.

I journeyed to Brazil with nine colleagues for the September 2022 meeting of the Mohamed bin Zayed Species Conservation Fund (MbZSCF). Created in 2008 in the United Arab Emirates, the Fund is named after the nation's president. It empowers conservationists to fight the extinction crisis instead of bureaucracy and red tape by supporting grassroots initiatives, focusing on threatened species in their natural habitats, stimulating interest in the natural sciences among young people, and attracting further contributions from around the globe. I was invited to serve as an MbZSCF advisor on mammal projects in 2011. Since its inception, the Fund has awarded nearly 2,500 grants to more than 1,500 species conservation projects. My colleagues and I meet three times each year to review and discuss grant applications, usually twice in Abu Dhabi and once in a remote location, such as this meeting in the vast Pantanal wetlands, where we are treated to a firsthand look at the successful impacts of wildlife conservation.

Among those joining me from MbZSCF on this trip was the one and only Russ Mittermeier, who is responsible for bringing me on board the organization. Russ, Jean-Christoph Vie (former head of the IUCN Save Our Species Programme and director of the Franklinia Foundation) and I review and recommend grants focused on mammals—except for threatened cat species. Feline proposals are handled by Jim Sanderson, founder and director of the Small Wild Cat Conservation Foundation. Olivier Langrand is our bird guy. Olivier's an ornithologist and world-class birder who directs the multi-donor Critical Ecosystem Partnership Fund at Conservation International. It's dedicated to protecting our planet's threatened hotspots of biological diversity.

Like mammal grants, those awarded in support of reptile initiatives receive multiple reviews. Allison Alberts, who recently retired as the San Diego Zoo's Chief Conservation and Research Officer, handles applications focused on snakes, lizards and crocodilians. Anders Rhodin, an orthopedic surgeon and chairman emeritus of the IUCN Tortoise and Freshwater Turtle Specialist Group, focuses his attention on—you guessed it—the world's threatened tortoises and turtles. Endangered fish proposals are scrutinized by Ian Harrison. A specialist on freshwater species, Ian has been with Conservation International for nearly 15 years. Invertebrates, with more than a million species described to date, are the largest taxonomic group considered for MbZSCF support and are currently the responsibility of Axel Hochkirch, an associate professor at Germany's Trier University. Regrettably, Penny Langhammer, a vice president at Re:wild who approves amphibian grants, and Mike Maunder, executive director of the UK's Cambridge Conservation Initiative and our go-to guy for decisions regarding plant and fungi proposals, were unable to join the group for this particular meeting and transmitted their recommendations electronically. As usual, the job of herding cats—keeping those of us in attendance in line—fell to MbZSCF Head of Fund Management Nicolas Heard.

The 10 MbZSCF participants present for this very special meeting in the heart of the Brazilian wilderness collectively have field experience that likely exceeds three centuries, yet only three of us had ever seen a jaguar in the wild, and I wasn't part of that lucky trio. For the rest of us, this was the opportunity of a lifetime, but we were up against the clock. We had only five days to cruise the Rio Cuiabá and the surrounding areas of the Porto Jofre region to spot the secretive big cat. The chances, we were told, were quite good, but no one would lay down odds for fear of jinxing the outcome.

THE MBZSCF TEAM EMBARKING ON THE TRANSPANTANEIRA HIGHWAY, BRAZIL, 2022

The morning after Rafael's dinnertime tale of an up-close-and-personal encounter with a jaguar, our entourage embarked on a 150-mile, four-and-a-half-hour drive to Fazenda Jofre Velho, the site of Panthera's Conservation Ranch. *Fazenda* is a commonly used Brazilian term: Portuguese for a large estate, ranch or plantation. The first hour and a half (on a well-maintained stretch of asphalt) brought us to Poconé, a municipality of slightly more than 30,000 people. After an obligatory pit stop, we transferred to the Transpantaneira Highway, which is really much too generous a name for that particular stretch of road. The next 90 miles, a relatively straight arrow of dirt that crosses some 120 wooden bridges, began with a somewhat jarring, washboard-like rhythm and massage, coupled with plumes of dust from our tires as we ventured into the wilderness. We had entered the Pantanal.

The Pantanal is the world's largest contiguous wetland lying mainly in Brazil but extending into Bolivia and Paraguay. The dynamic floodplain varies by thousands of square miles

JACARE CAIMAN ALONG THE BANK OF RIO CUIABÁ, BRAZIL, 2022

seasonally. At times, it can span an area roughly half the size of the state of California. A true wilderness, the sparsely populated region is home to some of our planet's most spectacular concentrations of wildlife. Within minutes of passing under the arches that mark the beginning of the Transpantaneira Highway, we begin to appreciate what's in store for the rest of the trip. It's the end of the dry season, a month before the seasonal rains arrive, so much of the marshland and savanna has been transformed into browning grasses and caked mud with much of the flat terrain sporting termite mounds that resemble earthen traffic cones. Where water remains, herons, egrets, storks and other wading birds scour the shallows for fish and frogs, while the larger species also roost and nest in the surrounding treetops. Banks along the roadside are lined with basking caiman or *jacarés*—a slightly smaller relative of the American alligator—many of their bodies touching, interlaced or even appearing stacked atop one another, while their avian neighbors walk amongst them, seemingly unconcerned. These scenes repeat themselves over and over for the next few hours

RIO, A MALE JAGUAR, RIO CUIABÁ BRAZIL, 2022

as we close the distance to our destination, counting wooden bridges as we go. Several bridges that had been damaged by wet season flooding are in need of repair, but we skirt them without any appreciable delay during these drier times.

Panthera's presence in the Pantanal is the result of its cofounder's dedication to jaguar survival. Alan Rabinowitz's pioneering jaguar studies began in the early 1980s in Belize, where our mutual friend, Sharon Matola, helped him with logistics while in the field. Two decades of research in Central and South America ultimately focused his attention on the jaguars of the Pantanal, a land he referred to as a "vast primeval sponge" and "an assault on the senses: fluttering flashes of competing songs from more than 600 species of birds, the eyes of thousands of caimans bobbing in the waters, and the subtle but unmistakable musty smell of scent sprayed from jaguars wafting from the trees." Alan's cofounder, Tom Kaplin, and the Panthera team launched the Pantanal Jaguar Project in 2006 at the nearby Fazenda São Bento and purchased the 25,000-acre Jofre Velho ranch in 2015 as a permanent base for its long-term jaguar conservation program. In addition to jaguars, other flagship species for conservation (all of which beg superlatives) include the South American tapir, giant otter, capybara (the world's largest rodent), giant anteater, maned wolf, jabiru (the largest stork in the Americas), and hyacinth macaw (the world's largest parrot). Overall, the Pantanal is one of the most spectacular and biologically diverse ecosystems on the planet, as well as one that remains largely intact and possible to protect.

Our team took a day to get settled at the birder's paradise that would be our home for the next five days. From the veranda of the visitors' quarters, we watched hundreds of small, green and ravenous monk and yellow-chevroned parakeets gorge themselves on thousands of nearly ripe mangos that hung from large shady trees. Beneath those trees and along the fences, pheasant-like, bare-faced curassows and Chaco chachalacas scratched for fallen seeds. A bit farther off, but still well within

BLACK SKIMMER FISHING ALONG THE SHORE OF A SMALL LAGOON, FAZENDA JOFRE VELHO, 2022

HYACINTH MACAWS EATING PALM NUTS, FAZENDA JOFRE VELHO, BRAZIL, 2022

view, small to medium-sized shorebirds—rails, sandpipers, jacanas and ibises—plied standing pools of water for bite-sized prey. A distant patch of hot pink marked a flock of roseate spoonbills siphoning the shallows with their long, flat bills. Meanwhile, larger, goose-sized Southern screamers screamed

MONK PARAKEETS FEASTING ON MANGOS, FAZENDA JOFRE VELHO, BRAZIL, 2002

JABIRU STORKS, THE LARGEST IN THE AMERICAS, RIO CUIABÁ, BRAZIL, 2022

as they patrolled the water's edge as aerobatic black skimmers skimmed the shoreline, their uniquely designed, longer lower beaks allowing them to scoop unwary fish from just below the water's surface. Above in the trees, the apex avian predators—savanna and black-collared hawks, tiger herons, cocoi herons and great egrets—either took a break from hunting or moved down closer to the river, watching and waiting for their prey to make that one last fatal mistake.

In our first morning meeting, the MbZSCF team awarded two special grants: one to an Ethiopian primatologist keen on protecting the newly-described and endangered *djam-djam monkey* in its high mountain, bamboo forest habitat, and another to a South African herpetologist whose organization is installing culverts beneath highly-trafficked roads to provide safe passage for the western leopard toad threatened by roadkills. We capped off the morning with additional grants awarded in support of a strategic planning workshop focused on endangered sharks and rays in waters off the Indian Ocean island nation of Sri Lanka; a search for Nigeria's little-known Ansorge lutefish (named after a nineteenth-century British explorer born in India) found only in the Niger River basin; and invertebrate conservation efforts meant to safeguard the future of the threatened black abalone of Mexico, red shrimp of Cuba, giant grasshoppers of Croatia, leopard crabs and sea cucumbers of Indonesia, and dung beetles of Vietnam, among others. Had the late Gerry Durrell been present, my money's on these words emerging from his mouth, "Well, esteemed colleagues, it appears that my 'Uglies' certainly have had their day!"

Our plan for the afternoon was simple. Following lunch, we would take a short break and then meet up at two o'clock to board boats for our trip upriver to find jaguars. At about a quarter to two, having smothered my exposed skin with SPF 50 sunscreen, and donning a cheap pair of sunglasses (I have a knack for losing anything approaching Maui Jim quality), I headed for the boats.

Two were docked a short walk from the ranch gate. Let me correct that. The boats *had been* docked only minutes before, at which point the Panthera crew received a radio call that a large jaguar had been sighted just a short ride upriver. Seven or eight of my colleagues who had shown up early jumped into the first boat as quickly as they could and took off. The rest of the gang then appeared, apparently while I was dawdling just around the bend taking photos of birds. They boarded the second boat as quickly as they could with no one apparently noticing that I wasn't present and, if they had, probably figuring that I was on the first boat. Well, you can imagine how pissed I was when I got to the dock and found not a soul.

At that point, I knew nothing of the jaguar sighting and just figured that I'd missed my first chance to see one in the wild. Bummer! I cursed the gods for my bad luck and was just about to wander off into the surrounding terrestrial wilderness with my camera when a young Brazilian field researcher named Raissa noticed me getting just a bit too close to a small herd of water

TI, A FEMALE JAGUAR, RIO CUIABÁ, BRAZIL, 2022

TI, A FEMALE JAGUAR, RIO CUIABÁ, BRAZIL, 2022

buffalo. She flagged me down from a distance, which I took as a warning. However, against the backdrop of the afternoon sun, I noticed the silhouette of a radio in one hand as she waved both above her head. Yes, she didn't want me to get any closer to the buffalo but, more importantly, I hoped, she managed to contact her coworkers about my situation to get me on another boat. And that, folks, is exactly what she did. *Muito obrigado* (Thank you, so much), Raissa!

That first day on the river, the seven MbZSCF team members who had yet to see a wild jaguar did so, even though I arrived some 15 minutes late to the scene. I believe the first animal was Ti, found lying majestically atop a mound of vegetation on the left bank. Perhaps a dozen other boats like ours lined the riverbank. The scene reminded me of lion watching on the Serengeti—just substituting outboards for Land Rovers—with monster lenses zeroing in on the subject and shutters clicking away in machine-gun fashion. Despite the crowd, there was an unexplained air of serenity, dictated, I feel, by the animal's demeanor. Ti, an adult female, has been observed on the Cuiabá River each year since her birth in 2015. She is a cub of Jeni, a litter mate of Juru, and mother to Guaraci and Alira.

I can recite these facts only because I purchased the 2022 edition of the *Jaguar Identification Guide*. The Jaguar Identification Project is a citizen science initiative focused on the northern Pantanal. Its founder, Abbie Martin, a biologist who hails from upstate New York, believes that giving a voice to individual jaguars is the best way to give a voice to the entire Pantanal region.

At the time of our visit, the Jaguar Identification Project, in collaboration with Panthera, had identified 99 individuals in the region of Porto Jofre. And that's in large part due to the excellent work Panthera is doing in an area with likely the highest density of jaguars in all of Latin America: eight of these cats per 100 square kilometers. In short, a relatively small international team of biologists has dedicated itself to demonstrating how local cattle ranchers can manage their herds effectively in a jaguar-dominated landscape and how a homegrown ecotourism industry can bring long-term benefits to the local communities. I believe this fits the definition of a win-win.

During our stay at the Jofre Velho Conservation

To identify

individual jaguars, researchers rely heavily on the spotted patterns of their coats, particularly of the face and forehead. Each animal's markings serve as a sort of "fingerprint" which, along with size, sex and scars, scientists can use very effectively to confirm an ID. According to the *Jaguar Identification Guide*, our group observed the following jaguars: Bororo, Juru, Kasimir, Krishna, Marcela, Medrosa, Patricia, Pixana, Rio, Ti and Tusk.

Ranch, my MbZSCF colleagues and I saw 11 jaguars, probably somewhere between 10 and 20 percent of the regional population. We watched as they basked in the morning sun, frolicked with cubs and hunted jacaré and capybara in the shallows, just their spotted heads visible within the floating green mat of water hyacinths on the surface. We soaked in the other wildlife as well, quickly losing count of caimans and waterfowl along the river, and waiting until the very end of our visit for the treat of seeing a giant otter catch and eat a fish. Hiking along a forest trail, we even encountered the world's largest species of grasshopper—and lived to tell about it! During our five days, we also managed to conduct business, doling out close to $500,000 in grants to 52 projects in nearly 30 countries—not bad for a week's work.

LESSON LEARNED:

This particular trip—the intertwined meetings and wildlife adventures—brought together all that is meaningful to me. If I can, I plan to spend the rest of my life working with friends and colleagues to help preserve and protect Earth's wildlife heritage, and I will try my very best not to miss those golden opportunities to experience these wonders firsthand.

GIANT OTTER, RIO CUIABÁ, BRAZIL, 2022

CAPYBARA TRIO, RIO CUIABÁ, BRAZIL, 2022

ME AS A WOLF AT THE ELMWOOD PARK ZOO'S BEAST OF A FEAST, PA, 2009

BILL'S BUCKET LIST

I plan to live forever, or die trying.

Groucho Marx

It's been an interesting couple of years writing this book with the world in the throes of a viral pandemic. I've spent a fair amount of time conjuring up memories of past adventures and contemplating those to come.

Here's to the future! My mom is 91, two of her brothers are in their early nineties, Little Grandma lived to the ripe old age of 98, and Big Grandma topped her by one, taking in this world until just a few months shy of her 100th birthday. So I'm thinking about setting a family record and surviving to 100.

With fairly decent prospects for longevity and a fine family with whom to share my golden years, I treat each new day as another roll of the dice and, sticking with the golden theme, do my best to abide by the Golden Rule. My one regret would be reaching the end of the line only to discover that I wasted time on trivial pursuits, got distracted by too many shiny objects and failed to stay focused on what really matters.

My dad set me straight about such things one summer day many years ago—the day he suffered a heart attack while at home with my mom. An ambulance whisked him off to the hospital, lights flashing and sirens blaring. I'm assuming that's how it happened since I wasn't there. I was incommunicado, finishing up a landscaping job in the Hamptons. My boss knew that I wouldn't be done until well past closing time at the garden center where I worked, so he asked that I just leave the truck in the parking lot, lock it and take the key home with me. So you can understand why I was surprised to see him still there, waving me down as I pulled off the highway.

"Your father had a heart attack! Get to Brookhaven Hospital as fast as you can. Leave the key in the truck and I'll put it away." Like a relay runner grabbing the baton for the final lap, I raced to my car, jumped in and took off leaving a long skid mark and flying gravel in my wake. For the next 15 minutes, there was no speed limit. I prepared myself for the words, "We're sorry, Mr. Konstant. Your father didn't make it."

I arrived at the hospital fearing the worst until I saw my father in bed. Yes, there were tubes up his nose and running into his veins, but he still seemed very much with the living and even managed a smile when I came through the door. Mom was at his bedside. She'd found Dad on the floor, dialed 9-1-1 and followed the ambulance to the hospital. We sat together for a while, she brought me up to speed on the situation and then took a walk to the cafeteria to get something to eat.

Mom wasn't gone five minutes when Dad looked over to me and said, "You know, Will, if that's what dying is going to be like, it really isn't so bad. I mean, there was real pain, but it actually was peaceful when that stopped. While I was lying there on the floor waiting for your mother to find me, I felt numb, not afraid. It may sound crazy, but I actually feel satisfied. I mean, I've had a really good life and done a lot of things through the years. I have a happy marriage. Your mom and I raised two good kids. We've had lots of fun times together. What else do I need to do?" He paused briefly, then finished, "If I die today, it's okay. I have no complaints. I need you to know that. I need you to believe that."

Dad was 50 when he had the heart attack. He eventually quit smoking, never suffered another and lived to the age of 75. There were plenty of times during the next 25 years when he didn't seem so calm or so content with life anymore, but we cut him some slack and got used to his complaining. The point is that the heart attack didn't cheat him out of doing anything else he wished to accomplish during his lifetime.

Applying Dad's near-death philosophy to my own life, I, too, feel content. Childhood fantasies have been fulfilled through real-life adventures, many of them shared with friends and relatives. Being content with one's life, however, doesn't mean one should stop planning future exploits. Should I ever question that premise, I just need to take a ride over to my son's house and ask to use the upstairs bathroom. The poster on the wall by the door reads, "Make plans as if you'll live forever. Live each day as if it's your last."

At 70 years of age with three part-time professional commitments, I consider myself semi-retired. For the past 25 years, I've served as an advisor to the Margot Marsh Biodiversity Foundation, created through Margot's bequest in support of primate conservation projects worldwide. As of 2022, the Foundation has awarded close to $15 million in grants and will likely continue for another five or six years. In 2011, I was invited to serve as an advisor to the Mohamed bin Zayed Species Conservation Fund. The Fund currently awards $1.5 million in grants each year. And just a few years ago, Global Wildlife Conservation (recently rebranded as Re:wild) invited me to serve as one of its senior associates, with a focus on primate conservation initiatives. Taken together, these commitments keep me well-linked with critical efforts around the world to save threatened species from extinction.

My experiences to date, as rewarding as they have been, only make me yearn for more of the same. And so I've spent a little time compiling my Bucket List. It's eclectic for sure, seems to be growing even as I write it and could easily take on a life of its own. Stay tuned ...

HIGH ABOVE THE YELLOWSTONE RIVER, WYOMING, 2014

1 | CLIMB MOUNT KILIMANJARO WITH MY BUDDY RICK BARONGI

2 | FIND THE FOREST IN ISRAEL WHERE A TREE WAS PLANTED IN MEMORY OF SCOTT, OUR FIRST SON

3 | CELEBRATE MY 50TH ANNIVERSARY WITH NANNETTE

4 | OWN AN ELECTRIC VEHICLE

5 | SEE A TIGER IN THE WILD

6 | RETURN TO MADAGASCAR AND SEE AN AYE-AYE IN THE WILD

7 | VISIT SAPO NATIONAL PARK IN LIBERIA

8 | RETURN TO PANAMA AND SEE GOLDEN FROGS RETURNED TO THE WILD

9 | SEE A JAVAN RHINOCEROS IN THE WILD

10 | SEE ALL THE NATIVE SNAKE SPECIES OF PENNSYLVANIA IN THE WILD

11 | WRITE ANOTHER BOOK

12 | READ 1,000 MORE BOOKS

13 | TAKE MY CHILDREN AND GRANDCHILDREN ON AN AFRICAN SAFARI

I have no set

timetable for these goals but may very well have to set that Konstant family record and live to 100 to complete the list.

GRATITUDE

I am deeply indebted to everyone who helped me bring this book—my first crack at a memoir—to fruition. My family encouraged me as I put pen to paper, as did many friends and colleagues who checked my recollections for accuracy. Sincere thanks are due to those who were brutally honest in their critiques of early drafts, providing essential, albeit sobering feedback.

Special appreciation is due to the staff and patrons of Glenside Free Library and the Free Library of Springfield Township. An adult education course offered at Glenside inspired me to cobble together the few dozen stories that comprise this book, a number of which received their first critiques when read aloud in class or shared with local audiences at after-dinner events. Thank you, Steve Dehlia and Abbey Porter, for joining me every few weeks after classes ended to hone our writing skills and dissect the results. At Springfield, my good friend Mary Lou Hughes invited me to join one of the library reading groups and invited members to review a near-final draft of *Wrestles With Wolves*. Their impressions and suggestions helped me decide what should stay and what probably needed to go.

My sincere thanks to those comrades whose memories of key events differed from my own. I found this to be fascinating. Thank you, Lee Durrell, for traveling back in time with me to reconstruct how you, Gerry and I walked away from a traffic crash that could have killed us. Sadly, too many of the people about whom I've written are no longer with us. I miss them.

Very little of what I've decided to share would have been possible were it not for the many organizations that sponsored

my travel to distant lands. The World Wildlife Fund, Wildlife Preservation Trust International, Conservation International, Philadelphia Zoo, Houston Zoo and International Rhino Foundation sent me to at least two dozen countries in Central and South America, Africa and Asia to help develop projects focused on saving endangered species.

I've filled the book with images and illustrations to bring you with me on these adventures. Most of the photos are my own or from the family album, but the stories would not have fully come to life without the images provided by a host of talented photographers and artists. And, for that, I am grateful.

A first draft of the book came into being at just about the time the pandemic shut down the world. That inspired me to send stories—one every other day or so—to fellow primatologist Jane Goodall, intended as bedtime reading during her confinement in the UK. I shared subsequent drafts with Allison Alberts, Anna Marie Lopinto, Russ Mittermeier, Anthony Rylands, and Hiromi Tada, all of whom offered constructive criticism. The initial task of the design fell to Anthony's daughter, Paula Katharina Rylands, who helped me whip the original manuscript into decent shape.

Simply stated, this book would not have seen the light of day were it not for the folks at Archimedes' Printing Shoppe & Sundry Goodes. Lucy Noland, Kim Gek Lin Short and Peggy Jackson tackled the final tasks of editing, design, layout, marketing and more. I owe this team a great debt for their contribution to the final product.

Most importantly, I am grateful to my wife, Nannette, who not only shared many of these adventures but suffered through my retelling of the tales again and again. And, as a reward, she got to read the final draft of each and every story which absolves her of any further commitment.